Developing a
Christian Worldview

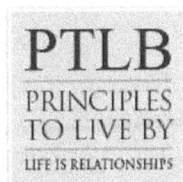

PTLB
PRINCIPLES
TO LIVE BY
LIFE IS RELATIONSHIPS

Gil Stieglitz

Developing a Christian Worldview

© Gil Stieglitz 2016
Second Edition

Published by Principles to Live By, Roseville CA 95661
www.ptlb.com

Cover by John Chase
Copyedited by Jennifer Edwards and Sandy Johnson

All Scripture verses are from the New American Standard Bible unless otherwise indicated.
New American Standard Bible: 1995 update.
1995 La Habra, CA: The Lockman Foundation.

ISBN 978-0-9909641-9-3
Printed in the United States of America

Dedication

This book is dedicated to those key professors who shaped
my desire to think biblically and theologically:

Dr. Gordon Kirk
Dr. Curtis Mitchell
Dr. Robert Saucy
Dr. Howard Hendricks
Dr. Francis Schaeffer

God used these men to help me put on the crucial
lenses of a Christian Worldview that allowed
me to see the world with clarity.

Table of Contents

How to Use This Book

This book is designed to be an intensive lay-level study of the basic teachings of the Christian faith. I will take you through five rounds of doctrinal exercises on the ten basic doctrines. Each round is a trip through the ten doctrines in a different way. They can be done daily, weekly, or over the course of a whole year.

As a personal devotional guide

Some people use this for individual quiet time to work through the material in which they look up the verses on their own, take notes, and develop individually. Usually when people do it as quiet time material, they take one chapter per day. Some have chosen to work through a chapter over a few days with no timetable for finishing.

As a small group study

Some have chosen to use this as a small group curriculum. There are a number of different ways to use this book for a small group. One method is to have each member of the group work through the material a day at a time and make notes so that every week they can share what they learned and experienced as they worked through this daily exercise. This always provides more than enough material to talk about in the weekly small group time.

A second way of working through the material is to focus on one of the rounds of material. The group is then asked to do the assignments in that round at a rate of one per week. The leader of the small group would then decide which one of the rounds to focus on for the group. Usually number one is most often chosen as it requires the most work in the Bible.

Another way to use this material as a small group curriculum is to choose two or three rounds to process through with assigned amounts of homework each week. How many rounds to cover would depend on the amount of time the small group has together.

For those groups that will be together over the course of a year, this material can be studied one week at a time and then discussed. This gives a much more in-depth look at the doctrines of Christianity and allows a small group to hear from each of its members from different perspectives.

As training and enrichment materials

Some have used this material to strengthen weak areas in their own understanding and foundation of the Christian faith. And some have used this for people they are mentoring or discipling to help bring them to a new level of understanding of the basic Christian doctrines. Used in this way, it can be approached in three different ways: 1) chapter by chapter working through the material; 2) focusing on a particular round and its questions and interactions on the Christian Worldview; 3) doing only particular doctrines in each round. This usually involves focusing on only one or two doctrines, usually those that need to be strengthened or developed in the person.

Introduction

When I was a sophomore in high school, I was sitting with a few friends in Geometry class. We were kidding around, and someone thought it would be a great gag for everyone to try on one guy's glasses to see how silly we looked. When it came to my turn, I had an epiphany. When I slipped the glasses on, the whole world came into focus. I could see people's faces clearly. I could see across the room. I could see what the teacher was writing on the board—all for the first time. For the next few days I followed this friend around constantly asking if I could borrow his glasses. With his glasses the world made sense at a whole new level. I could see the connections between things. I could grasp the details. I remember coming to a place where I had to make a decision about whether I was going to keep looking cool without glasses or risk looking goofy but be able see everything clearly. Seeing clearly was too wonderful; I was willing to look silly just to have the clarity of vision. I took the leap and told my parents that I needed glasses.

Examining Christian doctrine does the same thing. It gives you clarity about what is happening and why. It allows you to see your place in the world accurately. Yes, there are some restrictions on your behavior if you embrace the Christian Worldview; but it is worth it to have the clarity of understanding.

We all live in the world, but some of us don't care whether the outer world is out of focus and blurry as long as we are comfortable with what is coming into our private world. Other people, however, want to understand the world and see it for what it really is. They want to grasp the reality of the universe that they inhabit. This requires that you put on "lenses" that will bring the universe and our world into sharp focus. You must be willing to ask the hard questions and interact with the real answers. Every religion and philosophy of life proposes answers to the big questions of life. These answers are lenses for seeing our world.

All religions and philosophies must have answers for each of these categories. The nature of philosophy and religion is that it is trying to provide answers to the big questions of life. I have chosen just three religions or philosophies other than Christianity for the sake of comparison.

Category	Christianity	Islam	Naturalism
Ultimate Reality	God	Allah	Matter
Prophet	Jesus	Mohammed	Charles Darwin
Active Agent	Holy Spirit	Allah	Mutation & Natural Selection
Sacred Writing	The Bible	Koran	Origin of the Species
Why & What Is Man?	Man: Image Bearer of God / Sinful	The servant and/or slave of Allah	An Evolutionary Accident

Category	Christianity	Islam	Naturalism
What is Success?	Salvation: Loving God, Others, and Self	Submission to Islam	Collecting Money, Sex, Power, Things
Promoter /World-view Group	Church	Mosque	School System
Other Beings	Angels	Angels	Aliens
After Life	Judgment Day, Heaven, Hell	Islamic Heaven or Hell	None
End of History	The Return of Christ	Return of the 12th Imam	Super Nova

When the basic truths of Christianity are used as the lenses to view the details and relationships of our world, it all begins to make sense. A Christian worldview is only one of many ways of seeing the world; but it makes so much sense, answers the questions, and fits the facts better than any other system.

Every major philosophy and religion must ask and answer certain basic questions. These questions are what we need to know about reality if we are going to live by a particular system. I have come to believe that the Christian system is the most coherent and fact-based system that answers the major questions of life. These are the ten questions:

1. What is Ultimate Reality?

2. Who is the true prophet of the philosophy or religion?

3. How did this universe come to be and end up in its present form? What is the active agent?

4. What is the sacred literature?

5. Why and/or what is mankind? What is man's basic nature?

6. What is success?

7. What institutions are essential for an ordered life?

8. Are there other intelligent beings in the universe?

9. What happens after death?

10. How does the world end?

What is the Christian Worldview?

A Christian Worldview is the Christian answers to the basic worldview questions. These answers come from the Judeo–Christian material that informs the Christian Worldview: the Bible - both Old and New Testaments. One of the earliest ordered recitations of the Christian Worldview outside of the Bible is in the document called the Apostle's Creed. The early date of this document says that the Christian Worldview has stayed stable for over two millennia. This document answers all the basic worldview questions.

The Apostle's Creed

I believe in God,

the Father Almighty, the Creator of heaven and earth,
and in Jesus Christ, His only Son, our Lord:
Who was conceived of the Holy Spirit,
born of the Virgin Mary,
suffered under Pontius Pilate,
was crucified, died, and was buried.
He descended into hell.
The third day He arose again from the dead.
He ascended into heaven and sits at the right hand of
God the Father Almighty,
from whence He shall come to judge the
living and the dead.
I believe in the Holy Spirit, the holy universal church,
the communion of saints, the forgiveness of sins,
the resurrection of the body and life everlasting.
Amen.

Let us explore the Christian Worldview and the answers to the ultimate questions from a little different angle. The following overview of the Christian Worldview should help you start thinking about the key questions that will be explored in this book.

What is Ultimate Reality?

There is a Transcendent Being who existed before our universe began that we call God. He describes himself as an Eternal, Infinite, Self-Existent Spirit who is Omnipresent, Omniscient, Omnipotent, Immutable, Holy, Good, True, Longsuffering, and Sovereign. He calls himself Yahweh (Adonai in Hebrew) and displays who he is in four large actions in human history: creation, the Exodus, the salvation of mankind, and the Bible.

Who is the true prophet of this philosophy or religion?

This Transcendent Being has an only begotten Son, the Divine Logos, who became incarnated and introduced to this world as Jesus of Nazareth. He is fully God and a separate personality within the One God. The Divine Logos was a distinction the Transcendent Being made within himself in eternity past. He is the prophet, priest, and King of the Tri-Personal Transcendent Being.

What is the active agent of the Ultimate Reality?

This Transcendent Being has and is a hagios (completely pure and transcendent) Spirit that goes out from him and is himself a separate personality within the One Transcendent Being. This hagios (completely pure and transcendent) Spirit has all the attributes and divinity of the other two Transcendent personalities. They all reside in one Transcendent Tri-Personal Unity. The Holy Spirit extends two kinds of gracious activity to our world. One is called common grace, which is for everyone, and the second is specific grace, which is for those who believe in and follow the Transcendent One.

How did this world come to be and end up in its present form?

The Transcendent Tri-Personal Unity created this universe and our particular planet perfect, but allowed the choices of higher-level beings to have real consequences into this universe. The selfish and rebellious choices of certain spirit beings and certain human beings plunged those individuals, their progeny, and this planet into dysfunction and brokenness. This planet and its human relationships retain some aspects of it original perfect design; but it has become a place of selfishness, violence, and rebellion.

What are reliable sources of information?

This Transcendent Being has communicated accurately with humanity over thousands of years in many ways but most significantly and directly through an infallible, inerrant, written communication in the collection of writings we call the Bible. The Bible does not contain all we would like to know, but it gives us an accurate record of all we need to know to live a successful life, reconnect with the Transcendent One, and be in heaven in the next life after this one.

Why is the world and mankind both beautiful and dangerous? What is man's basic nature?

This Transcendent Being explains that mankind is a crowning achievement of his creation activity; but at present, since the great rebellion, all humanity is both good and evil. We were created as unique bearers of the Transcendent Being's image; but because of the rebellion and selfishness of our first parents, we are now capable of great evil. Every man and woman is rebellious and selfish and thereby cut off from direct contact with the Transcendent Being. Because of the continuing rebellion, selfishness, and disconnect, no individual human can redeem themselves.

What is success?

The Transcendent Being has explained that lasting success is relational—filling one's life with love and connection toward the Transcendent Being, toward others, and toward self.

The Transcendent Being knows that due to rebellion and selfishness, individuals are disconnected from him, from each other, and from themselves; so he has provided a way to reconnect with him and begin loving him, others, and self in healthy ways that lead to success.

This reconnection and reorientation to love is called salvation. It is explained and illuminated through twenty-seven different metaphors, illustrations, and/or components. This reconnection and reorientation to love and removal of the wreckage of the past includes significant improvement in life here and now and full realization of our uniqueness and abilities in a life following this life.

What institutions are essential for an ordered life?

The Transcendent One has created and declared that three institutions are essential for healthy individual lives: the family (a man, a woman, and children); the church (a community of individuals who believe and support a common worldview); and the government (a ruling group of individuals who protect the individuals and order the society).

Are there other intelligent beings in the universe?

There are other intelligent powerful spirit beings that the Transcendent One has created to serve him and assist humanity. There are at least four different kinds of pure spirit beings spoken of in the Scriptures. Some of these other kinds of beings have also rebelled from the Transcendent Being's rule over them and are our avowed enemies. They seek to damage, obstruct, and destroy humankind's return to relationship with the Transcendent One and our journey towards becoming a reflection of his glory.

What happens after death?

The Transcendent One has a fixed particular day in the timeline of this universe where there will be a judgment of everyone who ever lived. For most this judgment day will be after we die. During this judgment, all of our actions, words, thoughts, motives, and attitudes will be evaluated. Some will receive mercy and some will receive straight justice.

There are technically two judgment days that the Transcendent One has set up. One is where the Divine Logos will be looking for good to reward and praise those who have accepted his forgiveness and embraced serving and loving him. The second judgment day is where those who have rejected him and/or maintained their own kingship of their lives will be evaluated for any mistakes or violations of the Transcendent One's laws.

In the afterlife beyond the present life, the Transcendent One has affixed one of two places where eternal souls will dwell. There is a heaven to gain by believing in and following Christ and a hell to suffer in for rejecting the Transcendent Being's offer. Heaven will be bliss for those who have surrendered their will to the Transcendent One's will. Hell will be endless conscious torment for those who maintained their right to try and be their own transcendent being.

How does the world end?

The Divine Logos who became man (Jesus the Christ of Nazareth) will return to earth to end history, judge individuals for their actions, and set the world right. He will set up a kingdom and rule through those who have embraced his forgiveness and ruler in their lives.

Making sense of your world.

For over 3,000 years the truths of the Judeo-Christian faith have provided the basic structure to understand the world in which we live. A thorough grasp of the basic doctrines of Christianity provides one the understanding for life and reality. They operate like steel rebar allowing a person to withstand the storms of this life. There are storms because we live in a world gone wrong. Our world is a broken world—broken by the selfish choice of our original parents and even further by every other human who has ever lived.

At its core, Christian doctrine has been about the belief or embrace of ten truths. These ten truths help us see life as it really is. They are like glasses or lenses that allow the world to come into focus. It is the clarity that comes from these truths that causes people to call this a Christian Worldview. A Christian views all the events and facts of the world through the lenses of these ten truths. These ten truths have been handed down through the centuries as orthodox Christian doctrine. Christians can disagree about particular understandings of the ten basic truths, but all Christians embrace these basic doctrines or truths as the core essentials of the Christian faith.

There has been too little emphasis in Christian churches, schools, and ministries on teaching these ten truths. The Christian church has been chasing and teaching fads instead of repeating and emphasizing these life-giving truths. The Christian church must get back to teaching and declaring them. I invite you to drive the truths of Christian teaching deep into your understanding so you, too, will have a framework for understanding the universe, mankind, and life in general.

Round 1
Doctrinal Exercises

Day/Week 1

The Ten Truths of a Christian Worldview

What are these ten crucial lenses for seeing and navigating through reality? It comes down to what you believe about these ten essential Christian doctrines that form the core of what it means to think like a Christian:

1. God
2. Jesus
3. The Holy Spirit
4. The Bible
5. Man: Image of God / Sinful
6. Christian Salvation
7. Church
8. Angels: Good and Evil
9. The Afterlife: Judgment Day, Heaven, Hell
10. The Return of Christ

It's easy to see how the power of these truths can shape our thoughts and actions. Ask yourself the following questions: What difference does it make if there is an Almighty God who has and is currently communicating with us? What if there is a God who not only communicated with us, but sent numerous representatives and even his own Son to let us know what he was like and that he wants a relationship with us? Would it make a difference in how you live if an Almighty Judge was observing everything you did and said? Would it give you hope if you knew that the Almighty God has sacrificed enormously so you could be forgiven for your selfishness, mistakes, rebellion, and guilt? Would it make a difference if you realized that, yes, there is life after death? Would it make a difference if you knew that God was interested in a relationship with you? What difference would it make in your life if you knew that this life is a trial run for the next life? It is only as we see the world through these doctrines that we see properly.

Personal Exercises

1. Consider the ten key doctrines listed above. Which of them is making the biggest difference in your life right now?

2. Which of the ten key doctrines would you like to know more about?

3. The following is a pre-test of your present understanding of these truths. Think of three verses in the Bible for understanding each of these truths and record them below. I've given you a couple to get you started.

God
1. Exodus 34:6-7
2.
3.

Jesus

1. 1 John 1:1-3
2.
3.

Holy Spirit

1.
2.
3.

The Bible

1.
2.
3.

Man: Image of God / Sinful

1.
2.
3.

Salvation

1.
2.
3.

Church

1.

2.

3.

Angels: Good / Evil

1.

2.

3.

The Afterlife: Heaven; Hell; Judgment Day

1.

2.

3.

The Return of Christ

1.

2.

3.

Day/Week2

God

God is a Transcendent, pure spirit being. He is the creator and originator of the Universe, mankind, and our world. He is above, beyond, and before all things. The vastness of who he is cannot fully be comprehended by humanity. He has chosen to reveal himself in the stories and truths of the Bible. He is a pure spirit being without our usual physical markers of identification. He describes himself through his essence, his attributes, his nature, his names, and his major works. The information contained in the Bible does not completely explain God, but it is all that humanity can fully comprehend about him.

Personal Exercises

1. What do these verses tell us about God?

2. Write down five observations from each of these verses about God.

Exodus 34:6-7

Then the LORD passed by in front of him and proclaimed, "The LORD, the LORD God, compassionate and gracious, slow to anger, and abounding in lovingkindness and truth; who keeps lovingkindness for thousands, who forgives iniquity, transgression and sin; yet He will by no means leave the guilty unpunished, visiting the iniquity of fathers on the children and on the grandchildren to the third and fourth generations."

1.

2.

3.

4.

5.

Psalm 139:7-12

Where can I go from Your Spirit? Or where can I flee from Your presence? If I ascend to heaven, you are there; if I make my bed in Sheol, behold, you are there. if I take the wings of the dawn, if I dwell in the remotest part of the sea, even there Your hand will lead me, And Your right hand will lay hold of me. If I say, "Surely the darkness will overwhelm me, and the light around me will be night," Even the darkness is not dark to You, and the night is as bright as the day. Darkness and light are alike to You.

1.

2.

3.

4.

5.

Acts 17:24-25

The God who made the world and all things in it, since He is Lord of heaven and earth, does not dwell in temples made with hands; nor is He served by human hands, as though He needed anything, since He Himself gives to all people life and breath and all things.

1.

2.

3.

4.

5.

Exodus 3:13-15

Then Moses said to God, "Behold, I am going to the sons of Israel, and I will say to them, 'The God of your fathers has sent me to you.' Now they may say to me, 'What is His name?' What shall I say to them?" God said to Moses, "I AM WHO I AM"; and He said, "Thus you shall say to the sons of Israel, 'I AM has sent me to you.'" God, furthermore, said to Moses, "Thus you shall say to the sons of Israel, 'The LORD, the God of your fathers, the God of Abraham, the God of Isaac, and the God of Jacob, has sent me to you.' This is My name forever, and this is My memorial-name to all generations.

1.

2.

3.

4.

5.

Day/Week3

Jesus

Jesus is the second person of the one Almighty Triune God. He existed as the Divine Logos before he was born of the Virgin Mary as Jesus of Nazareth. His birth was the declaration that God loves the world. He risked his only begotten Son to redeem those who would believe in him. God was not writing off this rebellious, sinful planet and its inhabitants; instead, he was investing in its redemption. He became a man so that he could live a perfect life and then willingly sacrifice that life to open a way back to God for a sinful, rebellious, and damaged humanity. He died on a cross as the sacrifice for the sins of mankind. He rose again from the dead to prove his victory over death. He ascended into heaven and sat down at the right hand of the Father where he prays for us in our spiritual journey.

Personal Exercises

1. What do these verses tell us about Jesus?

2. Write down five observations from each of these verses about Jesus.

Isaiah 9:6

For a child will be born to us, a son will be given to us; and the government will rest on His shoulders; and His name will be called Wonderful Counselor, Mighty God, Eternal Father, Prince of Peace.

1.

2.

3.

4.

5.

Luke 1:31-33

"And behold, you will conceive in your womb and bear a son, and you shall name Him Jesus. He will be great and will be called the Son of the Most High; and the Lord God will give Him the throne of His father David; and He will reign over the house of Jacob forever, and His kingdom will have no end."

1.

2.

3.

4.

5.

Revelation 1:17-18

When I saw Him, I fell at His feet like a dead man. And He placed His right hand on me, saying, "Do not be afraid; I am the first and the last, and the living One; and I was dead, and behold, I am alive forevermore, and I have the keys of death and of Hades.

1.

2.

3.

4.

5.

Day/Week 4

The Holy Spirit

The Holy Spirit is the third person of the one Almighty Transcendent God. He existed with God and is God from all eternity. He is a person, not a force. He has guided and ministered to believers down through the ages. Since Jesus' life, ministry, death, resurrection, and ascension, the Holy Spirit comes to be with and indwell believers. The Holy Spirit has many ministries that he performs for believers and non-believers. He seals, directs, gifts, sanctifies, and regenerates believers; and he convicts, restrains, and judges non-believers.

Personal Exercises

1. What do these verses tell us about the Holy Spirit?

2. Write down five observations from these verses about the Holy Spirit.

Acts 5:3-5

But Peter said, "Ananias, why has Satan filled your heart to lie to the Holy Spirit and to keep back some of the price of the land? While it remained unsold, did it not remain your own? And after it was sold, was it not under your control? Why is it that you have conceived this deed in your heart? You have not lied to men but to God." And as he heard these words, Ananias fell down and breathed his last; and great fear came over all who heard of it.

1.

2.

3.

4.

5.

Isaiah 11:2

The Spirit of the LORD will rest on Him, the spirit of wisdom and understanding, the spirit of counsel and strength, the spirit of knowledge and the fear of the LORD.

1.

2.

3.

4.

5.

John 16:7-14

"But I tell you the truth, it is to your advantage that I go away; for if I do not go away, the Helper will not come to you; but if I go, I will send Him to you. And He, when He comes, will convict the world concerning sin and righteousness and judgment; concerning sin, because they do not believe in Me; and concerning righteousness, because I go to the Father and you no longer see Me; and concerning judgment, because the ruler of this world has been judged. I have many more things to say to you, but you cannot bear them now. But when He, the Spirit of truth, comes, He will guide you into all the truth; for He will not speak on His own initiative, but whatever He hears, He will speak; and He will disclose to you what is to come. He will glorify Me, for He will take of Mine and will disclose it to you."

1.

2.

3.

4.

5.

Day/Week 5

The Bible

The Bible is not a book about God; it is the book from God. God authored it through the men he picked to write it. He breathed his own spirit and life into this collection of books we call the Bible. It has been supernaturally composed and supernaturally preserved. It was written by God's direction over 1,600 years by different people. It is internally consistent and non-contradictory. It is God's message to humanity about himself, life, wisdom, and how to approach him. God made sure that the Bible did not contain errors so we could rely upon it when it speaks to us. It proves itself to be from God by writing history in advance. The prophecies that have been given and then were fulfilled are the watermark of authenticity from God. The Bible consists of the thirty-nine books of the Old Testament and the twenty-seven books of the New Testament.

Personal Exercises

1. What do these verses tell us about the Bible?

2. Write down five observations from each of these verses about the Bible.

2 Timothy 3:16

All Scripture is inspired by God and profitable for teaching, for reproof, for correction, for training in righteousness.

1.

2.

3.

4.

5.

Psalm 19:7-11

The law of the LORD is perfect, restoring the soul; the testimony of the LORD is sure, making wise the simple. The precepts of the LORD are right, rejoicing the heart; the commandment of the LORD is pure, enlightening the eyes. The fear of the LORD is clean, enduring forever; the judgments of the LORD are true; they are righteous altogether. They are more desirable than gold, yes, than much fine gold; sweeter also than honey and the drippings of the honeycomb. Moreover, by them Your servant is warned in keeping them there is great reward.

1.

2.

3.

4.

5.

1 Peter 1:20-21

For He was foreknown before the foundation of the world, but has appeared in these last times for the sake of you who through Him are believers in God, who raised Him from the dead and gave Him glory, so that your faith and hope are in God.

1.

2.

3.

4.

5.

Day/Week 6

Mankind: Made in the Image of God, yet is Sinful

Mankind or humans are two seemingly opposite things. The first element of humanity is that they are made in the image of God and are therefore wonderful, significant, and immortal. God has put elements of himself and his abilities into each individual human. Another distinctive of humanity is their material and immaterial make-up. Humans are different from other beings in that they are not pure spirit (like God and the angels), pure body (as are trees and insects), nor just body and soul (as are many animals and higher functioning fish and birds). Humans are body, soul, *and* spirit.

The story of mankind is the story of God allowing humans to make a choice to either serve him or try and become little gods themselves. The choice of the first humans, Adam and Eve, plunged the world into darkness at numerous levels. As the first humans, their choices deprived humanity of the perfection they were meant for and infected each individual through the generations with selfishness, rebellion, and imperfection. This resulted in the second truth element about human beings—that humanity is broken, sinful, and fallen from their original state of innocence. This brokenness, which resulted from Adam and Eve's first choice, has been furthered through the broken, selfish, and sinful choices of every other person that has been born on this planet. Before God ever spoke the universe into existence, he had a plan for dealing with this introduction of sin into his perfect world. He is committed to the people of this planet and he found a way to both rescue a broken, sinful humanity and honor his righteous standard of perfection as the entrance into heaven.

A long time ago I was overcome by the power of this Christian doctrine to explain and make sense of my life and this world. I was walking down a road in the Swiss Alps after hearing a lecture on the introduction of sin into the perfect world of God's original creation. The beauty of the Alps struck me, yet I had an awful awareness of the selfishness that lived in me and in others. For the first time in my life some of the pieces of my reality began to make sense. The truth of robust Christianity explained reality— sin had spoiled the marvelous creation of God. The world I was experiencing was not a perfect world. It had glimpses of the beauty and grandeur that God had originally created; but it was broken, dysfunctional, and twisted by the selfishness and sin of mankind.

When properly understood, the ten basic Christian doctrines allow a person to understand their world like no other philosophy or religion does. These truths don't explain everything about life, but they do build a framework to understand "the everything." The story of our planet is a story of Paradise gained, lost, and regained. The universe and our world were built for us, but we needed to be redeemed to experience it fully.

Personal Exercises

1. What do these verses tell us about Mankind?

2. Write down five observations from each of these verses about Mankind.

Genesis 1:26-27

Then God said, "Let Us make man in Our image, according to Our likeness; and let them rule over the fish of the sea and over the birds of the sky and over the cattle and over all the earth, and over every creeping thing that creeps on the earth." God created man in His own image, in the image of God He created him; male and female He created them.

1.

2.

3.

4.

5.

Romans 3:10-18

As it is written, "There is none righteous, not even one; there is none who understands, there is none who seeks for God; all have turned aside, together they have become useless; there is none who does good, there is not even one. Their throat is an open grave, with their tongues they keep deceiving, the poison of asps is under their lips"; "Whose mouth is full of cursing and bitterness; Their feet are swift to shed blood, destruction and misery are in their paths, and the path of peace they have not known. There is no fear of God before their eyes."

1.

2.

3.

4.

5.

1 Thessalonians 5:23

Now may the God of peace Himself sanctify you entirely; and may your spirit and soul and body be preserved complete, without blame at the coming of our Lord Jesus Christ.

1.

2.

3.

4.

5.

Day/Week 7

Salvation

Salvation is the act of God whereby he invites the unworthy and incapable sinner to begin a relationship with him through faith based upon the work that he did in the life, death, and resurrection of his Son, Jesus Christ. Salvation is a three-part process where God redeems the sinful person and makes them fit for heaven. These are successive and each requires large quantities of grace to utilize and complete. Salvation of the individual sinner started before the world began and will be completed in eternity.

Salvation is about being forgiven, accepted, approved, and rewarded by God. There are essentially two ways to try and accomplish salvation and end up in heaven. One way doesn't work and it is called religion. Religion is trying to impress God with our works, devotion, sincerity, and sacrifice. The other way to win approval with God that does work is the way of faith. Faith means believing God for his promises and grace to do what you could never do on your own. The New Testament goes out of its way to contrast these two approaches to God: religion versus faith; works versus belief. Christianity is not technically a religion; it is a way of faith. Christianity is a life of day-by-day trust in Jesus Christ and his work on the cross of Calvary.

The book of Romans in the New Testament details the contrast between these two ways to God. Religion tries to impress God with the individual's devotion, works, sacrifices, ceremonies, and dedication. Religion is called works in the New Testament. This method is about trying to force God to accept you because you are so wonderful or perfect or gifted or something. All the major religions of the world try and use this path to God. Unfortunately, it requires absolute perfection to work and no one is perfect. Even parts of the larger Christian church have become involved in religion instead of staying true to the way of faith.

Faith, on the other hand, realizes that you as an individual have nothing to offer the Almighty. In fact, in your present condition you are despicable to him. Faith is about trusting God that his way of acceptance, approval, forgiveness, and reward will work. Faith understands that if sinful humans are ever to be forgiven, accepted, approved, and rewarded by God, it will have to be God who does all the work. Faith receives what God has done and promises to do and then trusts in it.

The Old Testament is a record of various people whom God approached with various promises. He asked them to trust him to accomplish specific things in their life that he had promised. It was their faith (trust) in believing what God had promised that was counted as righteousness (Genesis 15:6; Romans 4:3, 9, 22; Galatians 3:6; James 2:23).

In Abraham's case, God asked this old man and his old wife to trust him that they would have a son. Abraham believed God could do this, and it was counted to him as righteousness. He was made righteous by his trust in God. He did not clean himself up and try and act better to become more acceptable to God (this is religion). He trusted what God had promised him and therefore God gave him forgiveness, acceptance, approval, and reward.

The Old Testament also tells us that David, the shepherd boy, was asked to trust that God would make him king of his country one day even though it was seemingly impossible. David trusted that God would make it happen. Through his faith God not only made

David a king, he made him bound for heaven through his faith.

In the New Testament, God is not asking us to trust him for different things; he is asking us to trust him that he has provided the forgiveness for our sins in the life, death, and resurrection of his Son, Jesus Christ. Look at John 6:28-29:

> *Therefore they said to Him, "What shall we do, so that we may work the works of God?" Jesus answered and said to them, "This is the work of God, that you believe in Him whom He has sent."*

We begin a life of faith in this present age through trusting Jesus Christ as our Savior and the Lord of our life. We do not have to wait for God to speak to us. He has already spoken to us in his Son. *If you confess with your mouth Jesus as Lord and believe in your heart that God raised Him from the dead, you will be saved.* (Romans 10:9). We begin with Jesus as Savior. It is in this way that we gain forgiveness, acceptance, approval, and reward from God. We are, through Jesus, introduced into this life of faith. God will ask you to trust him for other things after you start by trusting Jesus. The Christian life is a life of faith.

To become a Christian is to have faith that what Jesus Christ did in his life, death, and resurrection 2,000 years ago will cause you to be forgiven, accepted, approved, and rewarded by God. What Jesus did and your faith in it makes an eternal difference in your relationship with God. You must trust that what God did through Jesus really pays for the penalty of your sins.

The following is a prayer that can begin your life of faith in God:

Dear Heavenly Father,

I come to you through the work of your only begotten Son, Jesus Christ. I admit that I am a sinner and have violated your rules and standards in my life. I need your gift of forgiveness in Jesus. I right now accept his payment for my sins. I ask him to make me everything you want me to be. Thank You, Jesus, for dying on the cross for my sins. I believe in You as my only hope of heaven and eternal life.

Amen

After you have begun trusting God by believing in Jesus Christ as the only begotten Son of God and your only hope for heaven, God will continue to ask you to trust him in order to grow in your Christian life. The whole Christian life is a life of trusting God. We are not trying to please God by our works and efforts. We are obeying and believing God when he asks us to trust him in various aspects of our lives.

Personal Exercises

1.   What do these verses tell us about Salvation?

2.   Write down five observations from each of these verses about Salvation.

John 1:29

The next day he saw Jesus coming to him and said, "Behold, the Lamb of God who takes away the sin of the world!"

1.

2.

3.

4.

5.

Romans 3:21-27

But now apart from the Law the righteousness of God has been manifested, being witnessed by the Law and the Prophets, even the righteousness of God through faith in Jesus Christ for all those who believe; for there is no distinction; for all have sinned and fall short of the glory of God, being justified as a gift by His grace through the redemption which is in Christ Jesus; whom God displayed publicly as a propitiation in His blood through faith. This was to demonstrate His righteousness, because in the forbearance of God He passed over the sins previously committed; for the demonstration, I say, of His righteousness at the present time, so that He would be just and the justifier of the one who has faith in Jesus. Where then is boasting? It is excluded. By what kind of law? Of works? No, but by a law of faith.

1.

2.

3.

4.

5.

Romans 8:28-30

And we know that God causes all things to work together for good to those who love God, to those who are called according to His purpose. For those whom He foreknew, He also predestined to become conformed to the image of His Son, so that He would be the firstborn among many brethren; and these whom He predestined, He also called; and these whom He called, He also justified; and these whom He justified, He also glorified.

1.

2.

3.

4.

5.

Jeremiah 31:31-34

"Behold, days are coming," declares the LORD, "when I will make a new covenant with the house of Israel and with the house of Judah, not like the covenant which I made with their fathers in the day I took them by the hand to bring them out of the land of Egypt, My covenant which they broke, although I was a husband to them," declares the LORD. "But this is the covenant which I will make with the house of Israel after those days," declares the LORD, "I will put My law within them and on their heart I will write it; and I will be their God, and they shall be My people. They will not teach again, each man his neighbor and each man his brother, saying, 'Know the LORD,' for they will all know Me, from the least of them to the greatest of them," declares the LORD, "for I will forgive their iniquity, and their sin I will remember no more."

1.

2.

3.

4.

5.

Day/Week 8

The Church

The church is the creation of God that he uses to change the world by creating, providing for, and releasing believers into this present sinful world. It began at Pentecost with the giving of the Holy Spirit. It is for the growth and community of individual believers and the promotion of the gospel, God's love to the world, and the majesty of God. Participation in the church is a necessary aspect of a believer's spiritual journey to maturity. The church has five purposes for its existence: Worship, Evangelism, Discipleship, Fellowship, and Compassion. The true church is made up of all those who truly express faith in Jesus Christ as their Savior, Lord, and God. The church has local expressions around the world. As the individual believers gather together, they become the church, exhibiting a force for good. Believers are "salt" and "light" individually when they are collectively a part of a healthy church (Matthew 5:13-16).

Personal Exercises

1. What do these verses tell us about the Church?

2. Write down five observations from each of these verses about the Church.

Matthew 16:16-19

Simon Peter answered, "You are the Christ, the Son of the living God." And Jesus said to him, "Blessed are you, Simon Barjona, because flesh and blood did not reveal this to you, but My Father who is in heaven. I also say to you that you are Peter, and upon this rock I will build My church; and the gates of Hades will not overpower it. I will give you the keys of the kingdom of heaven; and whatever you bind on earth shall have been bound in heaven, and whatever you loose on earth shall have been loosed in heaven."

1.

2.

3.

4.

5.

Ephesians 4:11-16

And He gave some as apostles, and some as prophets, and some as evangelists, and some as pastors and teachers, for the equipping of the saints for the work of service, to the building up of the body of Christ; until we all attain to the unity of the faith, and of the knowledge of the Son of God, to a mature man, to the measure of the stature which belongs to the fullness of Christ. As a result, we are no longer to be children, tossed here and there by waves and carried about by every wind of doctrine, by the trickery of men, by craftiness in deceitful scheming; but speaking the truth in love, we are to grow up in all aspects into Him who is the head, even Christ, from whom the whole body, being fitted and held together by what every joint supplies, according to the proper working of each individual part, causes the growth of the body for the building up of itself in love.

1.

2.

3.

4.

5.

Acts 2:41-47

So then, those who had received his word were baptized; and that day there were added about three thousand souls. They were continually devoting themselves to the apostles' teaching and to fellowship, to the breaking of bread and to prayer. Everyone kept feeling a sense of awe; and many wonders and signs were taking place through the apostles. And all those who had believed were together and had all things in common; and they began selling their property and possessions and were sharing them with all, as anyone might have need. Day by day continuing with one mind in the temple, and breaking bread from house to house, they were taking their meals together with gladness and sincerity of heart, praising God and having favor with all the people. And the Lord was adding to their number day by day those who were being saved.

1.

2.

3.

4.

5.

Day/Week 9

Angels: Elect and Evil

Angels are spirit beings created by God to serve him and mankind. The Bible speaks of at least four different kinds of angels: Cherubim, Seraphim, Archangels, and Angels. Their purpose is to be ministering spirits to aid in God's plan of salvation and management of the universe. At the beginning of creation all the angels were in harmony under God's rule. But a portion of the angels rebelled from God's plan and followed a powerful angelic being. These angels are now called demons or wicked spirits. Their desire is to corrupt and disrupt God's plan of redemption. They control the systems of this world, and they seek to hide the wonder of God and his plan of redemption. Every believer is, and will be, tempted, disrupted, and attacked to keep them from fulfilling their full role in the story of redemption.

Personal Exercises

1. What do these verses tell us about the Angels: Elect and Evil?

2. Write down five observations from each of these verses about Angels

Hebrews 1:14

Are they not all ministering spirits, sent out to render service for the sake of those who will inherit salvation?

1.

2.

3.

4.

5.

Luke 2:13

And suddenly there appeared with the angel a multitude of the heavenly host praising God and saying . . .

1.

2.

3.

4.

5.

Matthew 18:10

"See that you do not despise one of these little ones, for I say to you that their angels in heaven continually see the face of My Father who is in heaven."

1.

2.

3.

4.

5.

Ezekiel 28:12-19

"Son of man, take up a lamentation over the king of Tyre and say to him, 'Thus says the Lord GOD, "You had the seal of perfection, full of wisdom and perfect in beauty. You were in Eden, the garden of God; every precious stone was your covering: The ruby, the topaz and the diamond; the beryl, the onyx and the jasper; the lapis lazuli, the turquoise and the emerald; and the gold, the workmanship of your settings and sockets, was in you. On the day that you were created. They were prepared. You were the anointed cherub who covers, and I placed you there. You were on the holy mountain of God; you walked in the midst of the stones of fire. You were blameless in your ways from the day you were created until unrighteousness was found in you. By the abundance of your trade you were internally filled with violence, and you sinned; therefore I have cast you as profane from the mountain of God. And I have destroyed you, O covering cherub, from the midst of the stones of fire. Your heart was lifted up because of your beauty; you corrupted your wisdom by reason of your splendor. I cast you to the ground; I put you before kings, that they may see you. By the multitude of your iniquities, in the unrighteousness of your trade you profaned your sanctuaries. Therefore I have brought fire from the midst of you; it has consumed you, and I have turned you to ashes on the earth in the eyes of all who see you. All who know you among the peoples are appalled at you; you have become terrified and you will cease to be forever. '"

1.

2.

3.

4.

5.

Day/Week10

The Afterlife: Judgment Day

There are three major aspects to the Christian understanding of the afterlife: Judgment Day, Heaven, and Hell. All of these together make up a proper understanding of the afterlife. There are three verses to explore for each concept.

There will be a Judgment Day for every person after they die. For those who have believed in Jesus Christ and his payment for their sins, their judgment will be one of rewards and responsibilities. God will look over their life for opportunities to bless and encourage them. For those who have rejected God's offer of salvation in Jesus, their judgment will be God pouring over their life looking for their sins, mistakes, errors, and wicked deeds. The choice as to which judgment a person endures is up to the individual.

Personal Exercises

1. What do these verses tell us about Judgment Day?

2. Write down five observations from each of these verses about Judgment Day.

Revelation 20:11-15

Then I saw a great white throne and Him who sat upon it, from whose presence earth and heaven fled away, and no place was found for them. And I saw the dead, the great and the small, standing before the throne, and books were opened; and another book was opened, which is the book of life; and the dead were judged from the things which were written in the books, according to their deeds. And the sea gave up the dead which were in it, and death and Hades gave up the dead which were in them; and they were judged, every one of them according to their deeds. Then death and Hades were thrown into the lake of fire. This is the second death, the lake of fire. And if anyone's name was not found written in the book of life, he was thrown into the lake of fire.

1.

2.

3.

4.

5.

2 Thessalonians 1:5-10

This is a plain indication of God's righteous judgment so that you will be considered worthy of the kingdom of God, for which indeed you are suffering. For after all it is only just for God to repay with affliction those who afflict you, and to give relief to you who are afflicted and to us as well when the Lord Jesus will be revealed from heaven with His mighty angels in flaming fire, dealing out retribution to those who do not know God and to those who do not obey the gospel of our Lord Jesus. These will pay the penalty of eternal destruction, away from the presence of the Lord and from the glory of His power, when He comes to be glorified in His saints on that day, and to be marveled at among all who have believed — for our testimony to you was believed.

1.

2.

3.

4.

5.

Daniel 12:2-3

Many of those who sleep in the dust of the ground will awake, these to everlasting life, but the others to disgrace and everlasting contempt. Those who have insight will shine brightly like the brightness of the expanse of heaven, and those who lead the many to righteousness, like the stars forever and ever.

1.

2.

3.

4.

5.

Day/Week 11

The Afterlife: Heaven

There is an afterlife that awaits all people. Those who choose to embrace God's gracious offer of forgiveness through belief in Jesus Christ's life, death, resurrection, and ascension will be ushered into Heaven based upon no goodness in them. They will be given eternal life in Heaven as a result of Jesus Christ's work on their behalf. Heaven will be a place of everlasting significance, meaning, and intimacy with God.

Personal Exercises

1. What do these verses tell us about Heaven?

2. Write down five observations from each of these verses about Heaven?

Revelation 7:16

They will hunger no longer, nor thirst anymore; nor will the sun beat down on them, nor any heat.

1.

2.

3.

4.

5.

Revelation 21:1-27

Then I saw a new heaven and a new earth; for the first heaven and the first earth passed away, and there is no longer any sea. And I saw the holy city, new Jerusalem, coming down out of heaven from God, made ready as a bride adorned for her husband. And I heard a loud voice from the throne, saying, "Behold, the tabernacle of God is among men, and He will dwell among them, and they shall be His people, and God Himself will be among them, and He will wipe away every tear from their eyes; and there will no longer be any death; there will no longer be any mourning, or crying, or pain; the first things have passed away." And He who sits on the throne said, "Behold, I am making all things new." And He said, "Write, for these words are faithful and true." Then He said to me, "It is done. I am the Alpha and the Omega, the beginning and the end. I will give to the one who thirsts from the spring of the water of life without cost. He who overcomes will inherit these things, and I will be his God and he will be My son. But for the cowardly and unbelieving and abominable and murderers and immoral persons and sorcerers and idolaters and all liars, their part will be in the lake that burns with fire and brimstone, which is the second death." Then one of the seven angels who had the seven bowls full of the seven last plagues came and spoke with me, saying, "Come here, I will show you the bride, the wife of the Lamb." And he carried me away in the Spirit to a great and high mountain, and showed me the holy city, Jerusalem, coming down out of heaven from God, having the glory of God. Her brilliance was like a very costly stone, as a stone of crystal-clear jasper. It had a great and high wall, with twelve gates, and at the gates twelve angels; and names were written on them, which are the names of the twelve tribes of the sons of Israel. There were three gates on the east and three gates on the north and three gates on the south and three gates on the west. And the wall of the city had twelve foundation stones, and on them were the twelve names of the twelve apostles of the Lamb. The one who spoke with me had a gold measuring rod to measure the city, and its gates and its wall. The city is laid out as a square, and its length is as great as the width; and he measured the city with the rod, fifteen hundred miles; its length and width and height are equal. And he measured its wall, seventy-two yards, according to human measurements, which are also angelic measurements. The material of the wall was jasper; and the city was pure gold, like clear glass. The foundation stones of the city wall were adorned with every kind of precious stone. The first foundation stone was jasper; the second, sapphire; the third, chalcedony; the fourth, emerald; the fifth, sardonyx; the sixth, sardius; the seventh, chrysolite; the eighth, beryl; the ninth, topaz; the tenth, chrysoprase; the eleventh, jacinth; the twelfth, amethyst. And the twelve gates were twelve pearls; each one of the gates was a single pearl. And the street of the city was pure gold, like transparent glass. I saw no temple in it, for the Lord God the Almighty and the Lamb are its temple. And the city has no need of the sun or of the moon to shine on it, for the glory of God has illumined it, and its lamp is the Lamb. The nations will walk by its light, and the kings of the earth will bring their glory into it. In the daytime (for there will be no night there) its gates will never be closed; and they will bring the glory and the honor of the nations into it; and nothing unclean, and no one who practices abomination and lying, shall ever come into it, but only those whose names are written in the Lamb's book of life.

1.

2.

3.

4.

5.

Revelation 22:1-10

Then he showed me a river of the water of life, clear as crystal, coming from the throne of God and of the Lamb, in the middle of its street. On either side of the river was the tree of life, bearing twelve kinds of fruit, yielding its fruit every month; and the leaves of the tree were for the healing of the nations. There will no longer be any curse; and the throne of God and of the Lamb will be in it, and His bond-servants will serve Him; they will see His face, and His name will be on their foreheads. And there will no longer be any night; and they will not have need of the light of a lamp nor the light of the sun, because the Lord God will illumine them; and they will reign forever and ever. And he said to me, "These words are faithful and true"; and the Lord, the God of the spirits of the prophets, sent His angel to show to His bond-servants the things which must soon take place. "And behold, I am coming quickly. Blessed is he who heeds the words of the prophecy of this book." I, John, am the one who heard and saw these things. And when I heard and saw, I fell down to worship at the feet of the angel who showed me these things. But he said to me, "Do not do that. I am a fellow servant of yours and of your brethren the prophets and of those who heed the words of this book. Worship God." And he said to me, "Do not seal up the words of the prophecy of this book, for the time is near."

1.

2.

3.

4.

5

Day/Week 12

The Afterlife: Hell

There is an afterlife that awaits all people. Consciousness does not end when our physical bodies stop functioning. Those who choose to embrace God's gracious offer of forgiveness through belief in Jesus Christ's life, death, resurrection, and ascension will be ushered into Heaven based upon no goodness in them. Those who choose to reject God's offer of forgiveness in Christ or seek to impress God with their own efforts will be judged for their sins and assigned to the place of weeping and gnashing of teeth. This place is called Hell or Gehenna prior to the return of Christ and the Lake of Fire after the second coming of Jesus Christ. Hell is that place where the souls of the unrighteous dead are separated from the graciousness and mercy of God. Hell is a monument to the selfishness of men and women who would rather be the captain of their own life in misery than the receiver of God's grace through submission.

Personal Exercises

1. What do these verses tell us about Hell?

2. Write down five observations from each of these verses about the Hell.

Luke 16:19-31

"Now there was a rich man, and he habitually dressed in purple and fine linen, joyously living in splendor every day. And a poor man named Lazarus was laid at his gate, covered with sores, and longing to be fed with the crumbs which were falling from the rich man's table; besides, even the dogs were coming and licking his sores. Now the poor man died and was carried away by the angels to Abraham's bosom; and the rich man also died and was buried. In Hades he lifted up his eyes, being in torment and saw Abraham far away and Lazarus in his bosom. And he cried out and said, 'Father Abraham, have mercy on me, and send Lazarus so that he may dip the tip of his finger in water and cool off my tongue, for I am in agony in this flame.' "But Abraham said, 'Child, remember that during your life you received your good things, and likewise Lazarus bad things; but now he is being comforted here, and you are in agony. And besides all this, between us and you there is a great chasm fixed, so that those who wish to come over from here to you will not be able, and that none may cross over from there to us.' "And he said, 'Then I beg you, father, that you send him to my father's house - for I have five brothers - in order that he may warn them, so that they will not also come to this place of torment.' "But Abraham said, 'They have Moses and the Prophets; let them hear them.' "But he said, 'No, father Abraham, but if someone goes to them from the dead, they will repent!' "But he said to him, 'If they do not listen to Moses and the Prophets, they will not be persuaded even if someone rises from the dead.'"

1.

2.

3.

4.

5.

2 Thessalonians 1:9

These will pay the penalty of eternal destruction, away from the presence of the Lord and from the glory of His power.

1.

2.

3.

4.

5.

Matthew 25:41

Then He will also say to those on His left, "Depart from Me, accursed ones, into the eternal fire which has been prepared for the devil and his angels."

1.

2.

3.

4.

5.

Day/Week 13

The Return of Christ

Jesus Christ came to the earth once as he was conceived of the Holy Spirit in the womb of the Virgin Mary. His first coming provided the crucial basis for the salvation that he offered. He is coming again to judge the world and to set up his righteous kingdom. The second coming of the Lord Jesus Christ will be spectacular and demonstrate that those who believe in Christ were right to put their trust in him. He will end the misery and corruption of the present political systems and disputes. His second coming will begin with a shout and a trumpet when the bodies of the dead believers will rise first and then those who are alive will rise up to meet the Lord Jesus in the clouds. He will return ready for war and judgment. He came the first time as a meek and mild carpenter, offering himself as the payment for our sins; but the second time he will be a Warrior King.

Personal Exercises

1. What do these verses tell us about the Return of Christ?

2. Write down five observations from each of these verses about the Return of Christ.

Matthew 24:29-31

But immediately after the tribulation of those days THE SUN WILL BE DARKENED, AND THE MOON WILL NOT GIVE ITS LIGHT, AND THE STARS WILL FALL *from the sky, and the powers of the heavens will be shaken. And then the sign of the Son of Man will appear in the sky, and then all the tribes of the earth will mourn, and they will see the* SON OF MAN COMING ON THE CLOUDS OF THE SKY *with power and great glory. And He will send forth His angels with* A GREAT TRUMPET *and* THEY WILL GATHER TOGETHER *His elect from the four winds, from one end of the sky to the other.*

1.

2.

3.

4.

5.

1 Thessalonians 4:13-18

But we do not want you to be uninformed, brethren, about those who are asleep, so that you will not grieve as do the rest who have no hope. For if we believe that Jesus died and rose again, even so God will bring with Him those who have fallen asleep in Jesus. For this we say to you by the word of the Lord, that we who are alive and remain until the coming of the Lord, will not precede those who have fallen asleep. For the Lord Himself will descend from heaven with a shout, with the voice of the archangel and with the trumpet of God, and the dead in Christ will rise first. Then we who are alive and remain will be caught up together with them in the clouds to meet the Lord in the air, and so we shall always be with the Lord. Therefore comfort one another with these words.

1.

2.

3.

4.

5.

2 Thessalonians 2:1-12

Now we request you, brethren, with regard to the coming of our Lord Jesus Christ and our gathering together to Him, that you not be quickly shaken from your composure or be disturbed either by a spirit or a message or a letter as if from us, to the effect that the day of the Lord has come. Let no one in any way deceive you, for it will not come unless the apostasy comes first, and the man of lawlessness is revealed, the son of destruction, who opposes and exalts himself above every so-called god or object of worship, so that he takes his seat in the temple of God, displaying himself as being God. Do you not remember that while I was still with you, I was telling you these things? And you know what restrains him now, so that in his time he will be revealed. For the mystery of lawlessness is already at work; only he who now restrains will do so until he is taken out of the way. Then that lawless one will be revealed whom the Lord will slay with the breath of His mouth and bring to an end by the appearance of His coming; that is, the one whose coming is in accord with the activity of Satan, with all power and signs and false wonders, and with all the deception of wickedness for those who perish, because they did not receive the love of the truth so as to be saved. For this reason God will send upon them a deluding influence so that they will believe what is false, in order that they all may be judged who did not believe the truth, but took pleasure in wickedness.

1.

2.

3.

4.

5.

Revelation 19:11-16

And I saw heaven opened, and behold, a white horse, and He who sat on it is called Faithful and True, and in righteousness He judges and wages war. His eyes are a flame of fire, and on His head are many diadems; and He has a name written on Him which no one knows except Himself. He is clothed with a robe dipped in blood, and His name is called The Word of God. And the armies which are in heaven, clothed in fine linen, white and clean, were following Him on white horses. From His mouth comes a sharp sword, so that with it He may strike down the nations, and He will rule them with a rod of iron; and He treads the wine press of the fierce wrath of God, the Almighty. And on His robe and on His thigh He has a name written, "KING OF KINGS, AND LORD OF LORDS."

1.

2.

3.

4.

5.

Round 2
Doctrinal Exercises

In this next round we are going to approach the ten truths of a Christian Worldview from a different angle and perspective in order to drive them deeper into your thinking.

Let's do a little bit of review since you have just completed looking up the Scriptures for each of the ten crucial doctrines. Please list from memory at least one, if not all, of three verses for each of the ten truths?

God: 1) _____ 2) _____ 3) _____

Jesus: 1) _____ 2) _____ 3) _____

The Holy Spirit: 1) _____ 2) _____ 3) _____

The Bible: 1) _____ 2) _____ 3) _____

Mankind: 1) _____ 2) _____ 3) _____

Salvation: 1) _____ 2) _____ 3) _____

Church: 1) _____ 2) _____ 3) _____

Angels: 1) _____ 2) _____ 3) _____

The Afterlife: 1) _____ 2) _____ 3) _____

Judgment Day: 1) _____ 2) _____ 3) _____

Heaven: 1) _____ 2) _____ 3) _____

Hell: 1) _____ 2) _____ 3) _____

Return of Christ: 1) _____ 2) _____ 3) _____

Day/Week 14

God

God is not flesh and blood like we are and cannot be described in terms of height, weight, and other physical perimeters. He is pure spirit and describes himself in the Bible through five different aspects of his being and actions. Let's take a look at the five different aspects of God:

His Essence

- Infinite - Genesis 21:33

- Self-Existent - Acts 17:24-25

- Spirit - John 4:24

His Attributes

- Omniscient - Matthew 11:21

- Omnipotent - Job 9:4

- Omnipresent - Psalm 139 7-12

- Immutable - Psalm 102:25-27

- Holiness - 1 Peter 1:14-16

- Righteous/Just - Deuteronomy 32:4

- Goodness - Exodus 33:19

- Longsuffering - Genesis 6:3

- Truth - Isaiah 44:8-9

- Sovereign - Exodus 34:6-7

His Nature

- Triune: Father; Son and Holy Spirit - Matt. 28:18-20

His Names

- El: The Mighty God - Genesis 7:1
- Elohim: The Creator – Powerful God - Genesis 1:1
- El Shaddai: The Lord of Hosts - Genesis 17:1-2
- Adonai: Lord - 2 Samuel 7:18-20
- Yahweh: I AM - Genesis 2; Exodus 4
- Jehovah Jireh: The Lord who provides - Gen. 22:14

His Works

- Creation - Genesis 1:1; Psalm 19:1
- Exodus - 1 Corinthians 10:1
- Salvation - Ephesians 3:17
- Scriptures - 2 Timothy 3:16
-

Personal Exercises

Name three of these aspects of the Almighty that are the most intriguing and fascinating to you.

1.

2.

3.

In the last year, which of these has he been for you?

1.

2.

3.

In the last week, how has he been showing up in your life?

1.

2.

3.

What do you need him to be in the next week and month?

1.

2.

3.

Day/Week 15

Jesus

Jesus has many names and titles. The truth is that he *is* these titles and works them out in your life. As you are sensitive to him and his work, you will sense his presence and understand how to respond to his being each of these things for you.

Personal Exercises

1. What three of these elements of his deity has he been to you in the last three months?

2. Circle the ways you can see Jesus being active in your life as you reflect back on the last three months.

3. After you finish reading them, go back over the list and put an X by the ones that you need Jesus to be for you in the next three months.

4. Pray and ask Christ to show himself strong in the ways you have just marked.

"I AM": John 8:58

From the Hebrew Old Testament verb "to be," this signifies a Living, Intelligent, and Personal Being. It means that Jesus is the living God, who is outside time, pulsates with life, and is powerfully active in that moment in your life.

SOTER "Savior": Luke 1:47

Jesus is the Savior of all mankind and the only way to achieve forgiveness, righteousness, and grace to approach God. It means that Jesus is offering himself for you to 1) forgive you, 2) energize you to live a life above what you are capable of on your own, and 3) connect you directly with the Almighty God.

JESUS: Luke 1:31

From the Hebrew "Joshua" meaning JEHOVAH (Yahweh) IS SALVATION. It means that Jesus is God and is offering himself as the way to avoid God's wrath over our sin and rebellion while at the same time delivering us into God's presence and into a relationship with him.

CHRIST

This is equivalent to the Hebrew 'Messiah' (Meshiach), "The Anointed One." This means that Jesus is the long awaited Messiah (Special Leader) of the Jewish people who would open a way to God for the Jews and for the Gentiles.

SHEPHERD OF THE SHEEP: Hebrews 13:20

This is Jesus looking out for his flock. This means that he cares, directs, lifts up, makes rest, feeds, corrects, and comforts those who believe in him.

MASTER: 2 Timothy 2:21

By virtue of his person and work in Creation and Salvation, Jesus is the Master of all, especially of believers. This means that Jesus will come to us as our master and direct us to do something for him.

KING OF KINGS: 1 Timothy 6:15; Revelation 17:14

Jesus is the King that is above all kings and political rulers. This means that Jesus will, at times, force political rulers to acknowledge that they must follow his laws and live by his code of conduct.

LORD OF LORDS: Revelation 19:11-16

Jesus is the leader that is above all leaders. This means that he will assert his position of supreme leader over all other leaders—vocational, governmental, familial, and personal.

BISHOP AND GUARDIAN OF OUR SOULS: 1 Pet 2:25

Jesus oversees our life pointing out what direction to go and which to avoid. This means that Jesus is actively leading and warning us about what is happening in our life.

DELIVERER: Romans 11:26

Jesus is our deliverer from the wrath of God but also our deliverer from current spiritual, mental, emotional, and physical danger. He is active in his deliverance of us if we will follow his lead.

ADVOCATE: 1 John 2:1-2; Hebrews 7:25

An advocate is a defense attorney who keeps us from being punished and jailed. This means that Jesus pleads for our release from the eventual penalty of our sins; but also he pleads against the current accusations of the Devil, the world, and our own mind. He defends us before the justice of God, others, and ourselves.

SECOND ADAM: Romans 5:12, 14, 15

The first Adam failed to be God's perfect representative; but Jesus as the second Adam, lived the perfect life and voluntarily gave up his life so that his righteousness could spread to all who believe. This means that Jesus right now is seeking to spread his righteousness through your obedience and actions.

CHIEF CORNERSTONE: Ephesians 2:20-23

Jesus is the first and crucial part of the foundation of a whole new way of approaching God. God wanted people to approach him in an accurate and appropriate way and that way is through Jesus the Christ. He is constructing a new Temple to God out of those who believe in Jesus as the Son of God and their Savior.

IMMANUEL: Matthew 1:23; Revelation 21:3-5

"Immanuel" means "God with us." Jesus is the full representation of God in human flesh, living among us. If we want to know what God is like, then look at how Jesus acted. He was not just a prophet but God in flesh.

FIRST BORN: Revelation 1:5

Jesus bears the special title of the first-born, which connotes the supreme position. It means that he is leader and ruler over everything that follows.

HEAD OF THE BODY: Colossians 1:18

Jesus is the director, leader, and coordination point of all the actions of the true Christian church. He is the head of all the individual churches and the head over all the churches collectively. When the church listens to his direction, it is no longer spasmodic and unproductive.

ROOT OF JESSE: Romans 15:12

Jesus is the descendant of David, the great King of Israel, whose father was Jesse. Jesus is the fulfillment of the promise made to David centuries before that his son would rule over the people of Israel forever.

STONE: Romans 9:33; Ephesians 2:20

Jesus is the stone, which those who are trying to work their way to heaven stumble over on their way to God. It is not possible to be perfect from our human starting place. God the Father has made him the Chief Cornerstone for a whole new way of approaching God—the way of faith. Righteousness is obtained before God through faith, not works.

CHIEF APOSTLE: Hebrews 3:1

All the apostles were sent by Jesus to tell the good news that there was a way opened to God that did not require perfection; it required faith in the one sent from God. Jesus was the One sent from the Father to us with the message of salvation; he was the message.

GREAT HIGH PRIEST: Hebrews 4:14

The great high priest of Israel made sacrifices for sins once a year to cover the sins of the people. He poured the blood of a spotless lamb on the mercy seat which resided in the Holy of Holies. Jesus is our great High Priest who made the sacrifice of himself by entering into the heavenly Holy of Holies to pour his own blood out before the Father as the perfect sacrifice for our sins.

PIONEER AND PERFECTER OF OUR FAITH, AUTHOR AND FINISHER: Hebrews 12:2

Jesus was the first of the way of faith and was himself the way. On the cross he kept entrusting himself to the One who judges righteously and that what God had asked him to do was right, just, good, and propitiatory. His faith was rewarded with the offer of righteousness to all who would believe in him and his name became the name above all other names.

LAMB OF GOD: John 1:29

In order to cleanse the sins of the people of Israel, a spotless lamb had to be sacrificed in the people's place. John the Baptist cried out that Jesus was the spotless Lamb of God who would be sacrificed for the sins of the whole world.

LORD GOD ALMIGHTY: Revelation 21:22

Jesus is called the Lord God Almighty and functions in the role of Supreme Ruler of the Universe.

LOGOS: John 1:1-5,14; Hebrews 1:1-3; Rev. 19:11-13

John the Apostle uses the term Logos to describe Jesus in eternity. He was and is the eternal Word. He is the distinct person within the One God who is the expression of the Triune God.

SOPHIA: Colossians 2:2-3

Jesus is described as the summation of all of the treasures of wisdom and knowledge.

ALPHA AND OMEGA: Revelation 1:8; 21:6; 22:13

This is the beginning and ending letters of the Greek alphabet. Jesus takes this title because, just as in writing, one uses the alphabet in order to communicate. You never need to go outside of Jesus for faith and life. He is all you need.

Day/Week 16

The Holy Spirit

The Holy Spirit has many different roles and ministries as mentioned in Scripture. Look at the following descriptions and verses below, answering the three questions as they relate to your experience with him.

Personal Exercises

1. In what ways has the Holy Spirit been ministering to you in the last three months?

2. In what ways has he been trying to minister to you in the last three months, but you have been resisting him?

3. What ways do you need the Holy Spirit to minister to you in the next three months?

COUNSELOR: John 14:26; Isaiah 30:21

This is the word *paraklytos,* which means one who comes alongside and helps. The Holy Spirit is the one who comes alongside us, counseling and guiding us in the way we should go. When we listen to the guidance and wisdom of the Holy Spirit, our life is centered in God's will.

COMFORTER: John 14:16

The Holy Spirit seeks to comfort us in our affliction with new perspective, new understanding, and new direction. Embrace his comfort by giving him your burdens and allow him to show you about your situation from his perspective.

BAPTIZER: 1 Corinthians 12:13

The Holy Spirit is the one who baptizes the Christian into the body of Christ. We are made one body of Christ through the work and ministry of the Holy Spirit. When our physical body does not listen to its head and individual parts act independently, the body is wracked by seizures. When we do not listen to the guidance of the Holy Spirit to operate in coordinated fashion with other Christians, then Christ's body looks spasmodic. Is he asking you to work with him and other Christians instead of just doing your own thing?

STRENGTHENER: 1 Timothy 1:12

The Holy Spirit promises strength to do all that Christ asks us to do. So often we understand what Christ wants, but we turn away because we know we cannot do it. Scripture tells us that we can do all things through Christ who strengthens us (Philippians 4:13). He strengthens us through the ministry of the Holy Spirit. Is he trying to strengthen you to do something that you can't do but he can do through you?

SANCTIFIER: 1 Peter 1:2

To sanctify means "to set apart unto its intended purpose." When God allowed you to be born, he had a purpose in mind for your life. It is that purpose in each area of your life that the Holy Spirit is moving you towards. He is trying to separate you from all the other possibilities, both evil and worthless, that keep you from fulfilling God's purpose for you. Is God the Holy Spirit moving you towards your purpose in life? Is he moving you away from things and activities that keep you from that purpose?

SPIRIT OF CHRIST: Romans 8:9; 1 Peter 1:10-11

The Holy Spirit is the representative of Christ. Jesus said that it was to our benefit that he went back to the Father so that the Holy Spirit could be with us and in us as his representative. The Holy Spirit prompts and leads us towards Christ's aims and goals. The urges to righteous living, developing the fruit of the Spirit, and using your spiritual gifts come through the Holy Spirit at the urging of Christ. Listen and obey.

FRUIT OF THE SPIRIT: Galatians 5:22,23

The Holy Spirit seeks to flow through us every day in order to produce love, joy, peace, patience, kindness, goodness, gentleness, faithfulness, and self-control. The fruit is for others who need a touch from God, but we get the benefit of having God the Holy Spirit minister through us. Is he trying to have a particular fruit pop out in your life today?

RESTRAINING MINISTRY OF THE HOLY SPIRIT: Genesis 6:3; 2 Thessalonians 2:6

The Holy Spirit holds us back from all the sin of which we are capable of. Is he restraining you from a sin you want to commit right now? Let him hold you back by moving you in a new direction.

CONVICTION MINISTRY OF THE HOLY SPIRIT: John 16:8-11

The Holy Spirit brings conviction to your heart when you sin. Is he convicting you that there is serious sin in your life that needs to be confessed and repented of? Do not harden your heart against the Holy Spirit. Deal with the sin, rebellion, and selfishness; or you will miss God's best for your life.

GOD'S CALL: John 6:44; Matthew 22:14

God drew you to himself for salvation. If you are not a Christian yet, then he is most likely calling you to repentance and faith. He continues to call you to follow the Lord's will and plan. He is also calling other people to repentance and faith. Be alert to those he is calling around you so you can be a part of their faith process.

INDWELLING OF THE HOLY SPIRIT: John 14:17; Romans 8:14-16

When you become a Christian, the Holy Spirit comes to live in you. You become the temple of God through faith in the finished work of Christ on the cross. Activities and thoughts that may have been okay before now feel wrong and dirty. Activities and thoughts that were weird and uninteresting are now exciting and interesting (like going to church, reading the Bible, loving others)! The Holy Spirit is trying to make himself at home in your soul and your life. Are you cooperating or resisting?

REGENERATION: Titus 3:5

When you believed in Christ, God the Holy Spirit brought you to life spiritually by infusing you with the life of God in your spirit. He gave you life, spiritual connection to him, and a new nature. He wants you to expand the reach of that life throughout your whole mind, will, emotions, and body. Are there areas in your life where you are resisting God because it will mean that some things from your past will die? Are there areas in your life where God wants to make changes and you are resisting the new habits, ideas, actions, and speech? Go with the Holy Spirit's new life within you.

SEALING OF THE HOLY SPIRIT: Ephesians 1:13

When you became a Christian, God the Holy Spirit placed his seal upon you. In fact the Holy Spirit himself is the seal. The fact that you have the Holy Spirit ministering to you in the depth of your being means you are a Christian and headed for eternity in heaven. Do not grieve the Holy Spirit.

GUIDANCE OF THE HOLY SPIRIT: Galatians 5:16

The Holy Spirit will tell us how to live and where the path of our life should go (if we will listen). He does not tell us what clothes to wear and what time to eat lunch, but he does guide us in the direction and course of our life. He directs us to do righteous things so that the desires of our sinful flesh will not turn us away from God's will. Are you listening to the directions of the Holy Spirit?

FILLING OF THE HOLY SPIRIT: Ephesians 5:18

The Holy Spirit seeks to fill you to overflowing with himself so that you would produce the fruit of the Spirit in every arena of your life. When I am filled with the Holy Spirit, I am controlled by him: and the natural overflow of my life is the fruit of the Spirit: Love, Joy, Peace, Patience, Kindness, Goodness, Meekness, Faithfulness, Self-Control.

GIVER OF SPIRITUAL GIFTS: Romans 12:8-12;
1 Cor 12:1-11; 28-30; 1 Peter 4:10-11; Ephesians 4:10-12

The Holy Spirit gives every single Christian a special ability to use for him. It may be connected to what you have done before you were a Christian, and it may be something totally different. Some people have more than one gift; but no matter how many gifts God the Holy Spirit gave you, one or two predominate. He wants you to use the gifts he gave you. We can grow in our ability to use our gifts so that we are more effective for Christ. Is he, right now, asking you to use your gift? Is he asking you to develop your spiritual gift(s)?

Day/Week 17

The Bible

The Bible is a deep, rewarding book full of promises to its readers. Read the Psalm below and take note of the promise attached to that particular part or type of the Scriptures.

Psalms 19:7-11

The law of the LORD is perfect, restoring the soul;
The testimony of the LORD is sure, making wise the simple.
The precepts of the LORD are right, rejoicing the heart;
The commandment of the LORD is pure, enlightening the eyes.
The fear of the LORD is clean, enduring forever;
The judgments of the LORD are true;
they are righteous altogether.
They are more desirable than gold, yes, than much fine gold;
sweeter also than honey and the drippings of the honeycomb.
Moreover, by them Your servant is warned;
In keeping them there is great reward.

Personal Exercises

1. Which of the biblical benefits do you need right now?

- **Perfection** (how things ought to be, maturity)
- **A restored soul** (tipped back upright after being knocked over)
- **Wisdom** (a triple-win choice: God wins; others win; I win)
- **Rejoicing in the heart** (joy in your soul)
- **Enlightening of the eyes** (understanding, a new perspective)
- **Cleanness** (forgiveness, purity)
- **Enduring forever** (lasting, heavenly value)
- **Truth** (reality, reliable, accurate, without manipulation, righteous, ethical, positive, beneficial)
- **More valuable than money** (better than investments and wealth and excess savings)
- **Sweeter than honey** (delightful, dessert, and energizing)
- **Warned of danger** (alerted to manipulation, traps, temptations)
- **Great reward** (benefits, blessings, enjoyment, production)

2. According to the Psalm, which section of the Word of God do you have to read and study in order to get those benefits you want?

- **The Law of the Lord** (The Torah, the first five books of Moses, the Ten Commandments, Genesis, Exodus, Leviticus, Numbers, Deuteronomy)

- **The Testimonies** (The stories of the Old and New Testament Scriptures. Right now, which character from the Bible are you?)

- **The Precepts** (The principles and specific actions directed for each aspect and relationship of life in both the Old and New Testaments.)

- **The Commandments** (The first and second great Commandments: You shall love the Lord your God with all your heart, and with all your soul, and will all your mind; and you shall love your neighbor as yourself.)

- **The Fear of the Lord** (The passages where God himself is displaying his majesty, attributes, personality, and wonder.)

- **The Judgments of the Lord** (The passages where God makes a decision about something or someone.)

3. Put an X by the one or two sections upon which you need to focus your reading, study, and meditation.

Day/Week 18

Mankind: Sinful to Redeemed

When a person embraces the salvation that is in Jesus Christ, they receive forgiveness of sins, a renewed relationship with God, and an infusion of a supernatural ability to live in God's way of love. They are redeemed from the way of death to life. When a person receives Christ, a number of wonderful things are declared about Christians in the Bible. It can take a while to believe them about yourself in a way that allows you to live them out.

Personal Exercises

Read what the Bible says about "redeemed mankind," and answer the following question:

1. Which five aspects of your new nature and your new life as a redeemed person do you need to be reminded of?

    1.

    2.

    3.

    4.

    5.

The Christian's Position in Christ

I am God's child. John 1:12

Having believed in Jesus as God, he accepts me as his child.

I am Christ's friend. John 15:15

He calls me his friend because he has revealed his plans to me.

I have been justified. Romans 5:1

I have been declared righteous through my faith in Christ's death.

**I am united with the Lord, and I am one spirit with him.
1 Corinthians 6:7**

I have been bonded to Christ in a spiritual union which is indissoluble.

I have been bought with a price. 1 Corinthians 6:20

I have been purchased at very great cost to God, so God sees me as valuable.

I belong to God. 1 Corinthians 6:19-20

God claims ownership over me so that he can set me free to live abundantly.

I am a member of Christ's body. 1 Corinthians 12:27

God has incorporated me into the mystical body of Christ presently operative on earth.

I am a saint. Ephesians 1:1

Because of my trust in Christ, God sees me as holy and set apart.

I have been adopted as God's child. Ephesians 1:5

I have been brought into the place of full privilege in God's family.

I have direct access to God through the Holy Spirit. Ephesians 2:18

I know that my prayers get through because of the Holy Spirit.

I have been redeemed and forgiven of all my sins. Colossians 1:14

I have been bought out of the slave market of sin and released from the ultimate penalty of my sins.

I am complete in Christ. Colossians 2:10

I have all I need because I need Christ. Together we are a perfectly sufficient unit.

I am free forever from condemnation. Romans 8:1-2

God does not condemn me because of my embrace of Christ.

**I am assured that all things work together for good.
Romans 8:28**

God is powerful and brings good out of all the circumstances and even evil that barges into my life.

I am free from any charges against me. Romans 8:31

God will not listen to the Devil's charges against me.

I cannot be separated from the love of God. Romans 8:35

Nothing can separate me from the love of God that is Christ Jesus. NOTHING.

**I have been established, anointed, and sealed by God.
2 Corinthians 1:21-22**

God has planted me firmly to grow in him. He has specially blessed me and marked me for heaven.

I am hidden with Christ in God. Colossians 3:3

My real life is hidden with Christ, and all I really am in Christ will be fully displayed when Christ returns.

I am confident the good work that God has begun in me will be perfected. Philippians 1:6

God has begun a process to make me like Christ and will not stop.

I am a citizen of heaven. Philippians 3:20

My true home is in heaven with Christ. I am out of place down here.

I was not given a spirit of fear but of power, love, and a sound mind. 2 Timothy 1:7

God has given me his Spirit to strengthen and empower me.

I can find grace and mercy in time of need. Heb. 4:16

Every time I need God's power, his favor, his forgiveness, and encouragement, it is mine in Christ through prayer.

I am born of God and the Evil One cannot touch me. 1 John 5:18

God gave birth to a new creature when I trusted Christ, and the Devil cannot touch that new creation.

I am the salt and light of the earth. Matthew 5:13-14

God has called me to help preserve what is right and good as well as to show the glory of Christ and how life should really be lived.

I am a branch of the true vine; a channel of his life. John 15:1, 5

God has connected me to his inexhaustible storehouse of energy, creativity, and power. All I have to do is stay plugged into God, and all I need for any assignment will be available to me.

I have been chosen and appointed to bear fruit. John 15:16

God chose me to be one of his children. I did not get in by mistake. He wants me to show the fruit of the Spirit in my life.

I am a personal witness of Christ's. Acts 1:8

God has empowered me to tell others what Christ has done for me.

I am God's temple. 1 Corinthians 6:19

God has established his eternal presence in my body.

I am a minister of reconciliation for God. 2 Cor. 5:17

I have been asked by God to tell others that he is not holding their sins against them because Christ died for all their sins. They must accept Christ's payment.

I am God's co-worker. 1 Corinthians 3:9; 2 Cor. 6:1

God has been willing to work with me to accomplish his will. He has in some sense restricted a part of his will to my cooperation. I am working with God.

I am seated with Christ in the heavenly realm. Eph. 2:6

Christ says that I carry the same authority that he has as the one seated at the right hand of the Father, every other being is under that authority including the Devil.

I am God's workmanship. Ephesians 2:10

God is working on me to bring me to completion until he is completely satisfied and ready to enjoy eternity with me in heaven.

I may approach God with freedom and confidence. Ephesians 3:12

My ability to approach God is not dependent on my perfection but on Christ's finished work on the cross. I have freedom and confidence in Christ to come to God.

I can do all things through Christ who strengthens me. Philippians 4:13

There is not a job that God will ever give me where he has not also supplied all the power I need to complete that job.

* (Based upon Neil Anderson's excellent work on breaking spiritual bondage through *Truth Encounters*, from lectures in his classes at Talbot School of Theology.)

Day/Week 19

Salvation (Ephesians 3:17; Romans 8:29-35)

The process of your salvation stretches from before the existence of time and our world until it is fully consummated in the New Heavens in the future. Your salvation moves through processes and stages. The salvation that is offered in Christ is about all of these things taking place in, to, and through you. Learn to use your salvation to glorify God maximally.

Personal Exercises

The following is a list of the various processes and stages of Salvation. Answer these questions by looking at this list.

1. Which of the aspects of Salvation do you really need to be aware of today and use this week? Why?

2. Which of the aspects of Salvation do you have questions about?

3. Which of the following elements in your Salvation are you not taking advantage of?

The Process of Salvation

Foreknowledge: God planned out everything before he ever brought the world into existence. He knew you before the world began when he was planning what kind of world he would bring into existence and on what basis he would give people salvation. He already knew everything about you.

Election: He chose to you during this planning phase of the world. He decided whom and on what basis he would offer salvation. If you have believed in him with a sincere and lasting faith, then you were one of the ones he chose. All Christian groups agree that God planned the world and that he himself decided who would be saved. There is some disagreement on the basis of his choice.

Restraining ministry of Holy Spirit: The Holy Spirit held you back from all the sin you were capable of and all the evil your society and community were capable of.

Conviction ministry of Holy Spirit: The Holy Spirit brought conviction to your heart that you were a sinner and needed God.

God's call: God called you to repentance and faith in himself. God drew you to himself. God reached out to pursue you when you were not pursuing him.

Faith: You trusted in Christ to be your way to heaven and relationship with God. Your continuing relationship with God requires that you grow in faith. You must be able to believe God for bigger things.

Conversion: He converted you from a child of darkness, who followed vain reasonings, to a child of light guided into by his truth and his love.

Spirit Baptism: His Holy Spirit baptized you into the body of Christ making you a part of his forever family.

Indwelling of the Holy Spirit: His Holy Spirit came to dwell in you. One of the greatest gifts that coming to Christ offers is the present indwelling ministry of the Holy Spirit guiding us and refining us.

Justification: You were declared righteous before God because of the life and death of Christ on your behalf.

Regeneration: God gave you life, spiritual connection to him, and a new nature.

Union with Christ: You were united with Jesus in his life, death, and resurrection.

Adoption: You were adopted into God's family as an heir of life. You have graduated from the foster care of the Ten Commandments and oppressive rules about living into full membership in the family of God where your rule is to love God and one another.

Sealing of the Holy Spirit: You were sealed with the Holy Spirit bound for heaven.

Sanctification: You are being set apart for God's intended purpose for you to glorify him.

Filling of the Holy Spirit: The Holy Spirit seeks to fill you to overflowing with himself so you would produce the fruit of the Spirit in every arena of your life.

Spiritual Gifts: The Holy Spirit gave you a gift(s) to build up the church - His body.

Glorification: The Lord finishes the job of salvation by perfecting you in heaven.

Redemption of the body: The Lord resurrects your body and perfects it, also making it a heavenly dwelling.

Marriage Supper of the Lamb: Believers are invited to a feast celebrating the victory of the Lord Jesus Christ with those who have also believed in him down through the ages.

New heavens and new earth: We enjoy serving God and dwelling in heaven with God at the New Jerusalem.

Day/Week 20

The Church

The church is the creation of God, which started on the day of Pentecost. Believers in Jesus Christ gather together to accomplish five distinct purposes: Worship, Evangelism, Discipleship, Fellowship, and Compassion.

Personal Exercises

1. Which of the five purposes of the church do you most need the church to be for you this week? Why?

- Worship
- Evangelism
- Fellowship
- Discipleship
- Compassion/Service

2. Which of the five purposes of the church do you most need the church to be for your family or friends this week? Who and in what way?

- Worship
- Evangelism
- Fellowship
- Discipleship
- Compassion/Service

3. Which of the five purposes does your church need to focus on this next year to be healthier and vibrant? Why?

- Worship
- Evangelism
- Fellowship
- Discipleship
- Compassion/Service

Day/Week 21

Angels: Elect and Evil

There are two kinds of angels: good and evil. One kind is sent to help us, and the other is actively seeking to keep us from enjoying the full benefit of God's will.

Personal Exercises

In 2 Corinthians 2:10-11, the Apostle Paul tells the Corinthians to forgive a lapsed brother because otherwise it would be easy to fall into a scheme of Satan. What are the schemes of Satan? God has told us all of the ways that the Devil tries to mess up our lives in the Bible. Read the following descriptions and look up the verses given. Finish by answering the following questions below.

1. Ask God to make you alert to the schemes of Satan that the Devil is using on you right now and how to combat them. How is he trying to attack you? What schemes is he using on you? Go through each one and see if he is working on you.

2. Ask God to protect you from specific techniques the Devil is using to lead you astray.

3. Ask God to protect your family and friends from the techniques that the Devil is using against them.

Names & Titles of the Devil

Lucifer: Isaiah 14:12

He will entice you to ignore truth, relationships, and ethics to gain the beautiful or the brilliant.

Satan: Job 1

He will oppose you, block you, and become your Adversary. His opposition takes the form of fear, doubt, people, sarcasm, peer pressure, worry, etc.

The Devil: 1 Peter 5:8

He accuses and slanders you to others, yourself, and God.

Tempter: Matthew 4:3

He entices and distracts you away from God's best.

Roaring Lion: 1 Peter 5:8

He wants to scare, intimidate, and bring fear.

Belial: 2 Corinthians 6:15

He wants you to spend time doing worthless things.

Deceiver: Revelation 12:9

He is the master at deception and manipulation.

Father of Lies: John 8

He lies and makes false promises. He is always promising things that are not true or will never happen.

Murder: John 8:44

He uses violence and threats to get his way.

Sinner: 1 John 3:8

He wants you to break God's laws.

Beelzebub: Matthew 12:24

He wants you to enjoy a dirty lifestyle, actions, and habits.

Enemy: Matthew 13:39

He opposes your righteous ideas and actions.

Evil One: Matthew 13:38-39

He loves the wicked, perverse, and vile.

Angel of Light: 2 Corinthians 11:13-14

He appears as a supernatural messenger giving anti-biblical ideas and advice.

God of the World: 2 Corinthians 4:4

He wants you to value and seek after the wrong actions, words, habits, and lifestyles.

The Dragon: Revelation 13

He tries to terrify and intimidate you.

The Snake: Genesis 3

He indirectly wants to influence you away from God's best.

Prince of the Power of the Air: Ephesians 2:1-2

He uses demons to tempt, obstruct, warn, and distract you.

Ruler of this World: John 17

He can and does use governments and nations to persecute Christians.

The Wicked One: Matthew 13:19; Ephesians 6:16

He wants you to live outside of God's moral standards and think it is a good thing.

Day/Week 22

The Afterlife: Judgment Day

Personal Exercises

Read the Scriptures about Judgment Day and determine what God bases his judgments on. Then answer the questions that follow.

Hebrews 9:27

And inasmuch as it is appointed for men to die once and after this comes judgment,

Revelation 20:11-15

Then I saw a great white throne and Him who sat upon it, from whose presence earth and heaven fled away, and no place was found for them. And I saw the dead, the great and the small, standing before the throne, and books were opened; and another book was opened, which is the book of life; and the dead were judged from the things which were written in the books, according to their deeds. And the sea gave up the dead which were in it, and death and Hades gave up the dead which were in them; and they were judged, every one of them according to their deeds. Then death and Hades were thrown into the lake of fire. This is the second death, the lake of fire. And if anyone's name was not found written in the book of life, he was thrown into the lake of fire.

2 Corinthians 5:10

For we must all appear before the judgment seat of Christ, so that each one may be recompensed for his deeds in the body, according to what he has done, whether good or bad.

1 Corinthians 3:9-15

For we are God's fellow workers; you are God's field, God's building. According to the grace of God which was given to me, like a wise master builder I laid a foundation, and another is building on it. But each man must be careful how he builds on it. For no man can lay a foundation other than the one which is laid, which is Jesus Christ. Now if any man builds on the foundation with gold, silver, precious stones, wood, hay, straw, each man's work will become evident; for the day will show it because it is to be revealed with fire, and the fire itself will test the quality of each man's work. If any man's work which he has built on it remains, he will receive a reward. If any man's work is burned up, he will suffer loss; but he himself will be saved, yet so as through fire.

John 3:16-19

For God so loved the world, that He gave His only begotten Son, that whoever believes in Him shall not perish, but have eternal life. For God did not send the Son into the world to judge the world, but that the world might be saved through Him. He who believes in Him is not judged; he who does not believe has been judged already, because he has not believed in the name of the only begotten Son of God. This is the judgment, that the Light has come into the world, and men loved the darkness rather than the Light, for their deeds were evil.

Matthew 25:14-30

For it is just like a man about to go on a journey, who called his own slaves and entrusted his possessions to them. To one he gave five talents, to another, two, and to another, one, each according to his own ability; and he went on his journey. Immediately the one who had received the five talents went and traded with them, and gained five more talents. In the same manner the one who had received the two talents gained two more. But he who received the one talent went away, and dug a hole in the ground and hid his master's money. Now after a long time the master of those slaves came and settled accounts with them. The one who had received the five talents came up and brought five more talents, saying, 'Master, you entrusted five talents to me. See, I have gained five more talents.' His master said to him, 'Well done, good and faithful slave. You were faithful with a few things, I will put you in charge of many things; enter into the joy of your master.' Also the one who had received the two talents came up and said, 'Master, you entrusted two talents to me. See, I have gained two more talents.' His master said to him, 'Well done, good and faithful slave. You were faithful with a few things, I will put you in charge of many things; enter into the joy of your master.' And the one also who had received the one talent came up and said, 'Master, I knew you to be a hard man, reaping where you did not sow and gathering where you scattered no seed. And I was afraid, and went away and hid your talent in the ground. See, you have what is yours.' But his master answered and said to him, 'You wicked, lazy slave, you knew that I reap where I did not sow and gather where I scattered no seed. Then you ought to have put my money in the bank, and on my arrival I would have received my money back with interest. Therefore take away the talent from him, and give it to the one who has the ten talents.' For to everyone who has, more shall be given, and he will have an abundance; but from the one who does not have, even what he does have shall be taken away. Throw out the worthless slave into the outer darkness; in that place there will be weeping and gnashing of teeth.

1. After we die, there is a judgment of our life about what we did. Everyone will get a thorough life review.

   • What are the most significant things that will be recorded on the "tape" of your life?

   • Who will be the judge over everyone's life?

   • Will anyone escape a review of life?

   • Will any rank, privilege, money, wealth, or power exclude you from this judgment?

   • What will people be judged for?

   • Is this done privately or publicly?

   • Will people be judged differently? Based on what?

2. Revelation 22:1-10 says that believers in heaven will still serve God. The word serve is the same word used for worship in other parts of the Bible. So some

commentators and Bible teachers have suggested that heaven will be an everlasting worship concert. But eventually that sounds boring to almost everyone. It is only if the word means service does heaven make sense. Heaven is not an endless concert but instead endless well-fitted responsibilities that please God and advance his mission throughout the universe. God's servants will serve him by doing interesting, exciting, and significant assignments.

Our time here on earth is what qualifies us for various jobs and responsibilities in heaven. The more faith, love, joy, humility, etc., that we show here out of Christ's strength, the more responsibilities we will have there. God is watching us, as are the angels (2 Corinthians 12:19; 1 Thessalonians 1:3; 1 Timothy 2:3; 1 Timothy 6:13; James 1:27; 2 Timothy 2:14, 4:1; 1 Peter 2:4, 3:4; Revelation 3:1-2). Everything is being recorded in some way so that you can be rewarded accurately for your faith and love.

- What have you done in the last month that shows faith in God, love for God, or love for your fellow man?

3. The economy of heaven is built upon faith, service, and obedience to the Lord. It is not built upon money, power, wealth, and prestige as it is here.

    - How well are you being obedient and doing those things God has asked you to do?

4. We cannot take anything that we have amassed here in this life into the next one. We can only take who we have become—what our souls have stored.

- How much responsibility can God trust us with based upon how loving, merciful, righteous, peace-oriented, meek, and broken we have become?

- What are some things we are amassing or spending excessive time doing that aren't worth anything in God's economy?

5. God does not reward based upon how many people we've converted, the amount of money we earn, or the fence boards we have painted. He rewards those who diligently serve him. He rewards those who have allowed his Holy Spirit to flow through them and produce the fruit of the Spirit in their life for the good of others: Love, Joy, Peace, Patience, Kindness, Goodness, Meekness, Faithfulness, Self-Control.

   - What kinds of things do you think you will be rewarded for?

Day/Week 23

The Afterlife: Heaven

Personal Exercises

Read through the description of Heaven below. Mark five specific aspects of heaven that are the most encouraging. Write down why.

Description of Heaven
(Revelations 21:1-22:5)

- New - everything is new rather than old and worn out.
- A Holy City - separated from sin and selfishness.
- A New City of Peace - the New Jerusalem.
- Comes from God.
- Like a bride ready for her husband on their wedding day.
- God lives among men.
- All believers are his people.
- God wipes away every tear.
- There is no longer any death.

- There is no longer any mourning.
- There is no longer any crying.
- There is no longer any pain (physical, emotional, spiritual, mental).
- Heaven is free to everyone who thirsts.
- It is full of the water of life without cost.
- You must overcome much in this world to inherit heaven.
- There are no cowardly, unbelieving, abominable, murderers, immoral, sorcery, idolatries, and liars.
- God's glory is in heaven.
- Twelve is a repeating theme in heaven.
- There are twelve gates.
- Each gate is a single pearl.
- It has costly stones as foundation stones.
- There is no temple in heaven.
- Residents in heaven can go to earth.
- There will still be national identifications in heaven.
- Nothing unclean will enter heaven.
- There is a river of the water of life running through the middle of heaven.
- There are fruit trees blooming year around with twelve different kinds of fruit.
- The leaves of the trees have healing properties.
- There is no longer any curse on the earth.
- God's servants will serve God doing interesting and significant assignments.
- God will be visibly present.

- God's people will be clearly marked and designated as his people.
- There will be no more night.
- The light in heaven will not come from the sun but from God himself.
- Each of God's servants will rule and reign with God in heaven.

Which five did you pick? Write a sentence or two explaining why these are so meaningful to you.

1. _____
_____
_____

2. _____
_____
_____

3. _____
_____
_____

4. _____
_____
_____

5. _____
_____
_____

Day/Week 24

The Afterlife: Hell and the Lake of Fire

There are two places in the Scripture that are the place of the unrighteous dead: one is called Hell, Hades, Gehenna, or Tartarus, and the other is called the Lake of Fire. The first (Hell, Hades, Gehenna, or Tartarus) is the temporary abode of the unrighteous dead, and the other (the Lake of Fire) is the permanent abode of the unrighteous dead.

Personal Exercises

Read the following Scriptures and write down 15 points about what you learned about Hell and the Lake of Fire from them.

Luke 16:19-31

"Now there was a rich man, and he habitually dressed in purple and fine linen, joyously living in splendor every day. And a poor man named Lazarus was laid at his gate, covered with sores, and longing to be fed with the crumbs which were falling from the rich man's table; besides, even the dogs were coming and licking his sores. Now the poor man died and was carried away by the angels to Abraham's bosom; and the rich man also died and was buried. In Hades he lifted up his eyes, being in torment, and saw Abraham far away and Lazarus in his bosom. And he cried out and said, 'Father Abraham, have mercy on me, and send Lazarus so that he may dip the tip of his finger in water and cool off my

tongue, for I am in agony in this flame.' But Abraham said, 'Child, remember that during your life you received your good things, and likewise Lazarus bad things; but now he is being comforted here, and you are in agony. 'And besides all this, between us and you there is a great chasm fixed, so that those who wish to come over from here to you will not be able, and that none may cross over from there to us.' And he said, 'Then I beg you, father, that you send him to my father's house— for I have five brothers—in order that he may warn them, so that they will not also come to this place of torment.' But Abraham said, 'They have Moses and the Prophets; let them hear them.' But he said, 'No, father Abraham, but if someone goes to them from the dead, they will repent!' But he said to him, 'If they do not listen to Moses and the Prophets, they will not be persuaded even if someone rises from the dead.'

Revelation 21:6-9

Then He said to me, It is done. I am the Alpha and the Omega, the beginning and the end. I will give to the one who thirsts from the spring of the water of life without cost. He who overcomes will inherit these things, and I will be his God and he will be My son. But for the cowardly and unbelieving and abominable and murderers and immoral persons and sorcerers and idolaters and all liars, their part will be in the lake that burns with fire and brimstone, which is the second death." Then one of the seven angels who had the seven bowls full of the seven last plagues came and spoke with me, saying, "Come here, I will show you the bride, the wife of the Lamb."

Matthew 25:41

Then He will also say to those on His left, 'Depart from Me, accursed ones, into the eternal fire which has been prepared for the devil and his angels.'

What are some things that you learned about Hell?

1.

2.

3.

4.

5.

6.

7.

8.

9.

10.

11.

12.

13.

14.

15.

Day/Week 25

The Return of Christ

The Scriptures tell us that the Return of the Lord will be unexpected by the world but signaled with a loud shout and a trumpet blast.

Personal Exercises

Think about if you were given advanced warning that Christ was going to begin the process of his return next Friday. Read the following questions and write down your answers.

1. Would you add anything to your schedule?

   •

   •

   •

   •

   •

2. Would you stop doing anything that you are currently doing or planning to do?

-

-

-

-

-

3. The Return of Christ means a number of things. Read the following Scriptures about Christ's return and answer the following questions.

1 Thessalonians 4:13-18

But we do not want you to be uninformed, brethren, about those who are asleep, so that you will not grieve as do the rest who have no hope. For if we believe that Jesus died and rose again, even so God will bring with Him those who have fallen asleep in Jesus. For this we say to you by the word of the Lord, that we who are alive and remain until the coming of the Lord, will not precede those who have fallen asleep. For the Lord Himself will descend from heaven with a shout, with the voice of the archangel and with the trumpet of God, and the dead in Christ will rise first. Then we who are alive and remain will be caught up together with them in the clouds to meet the Lord in the air, and so we shall always be with the Lord. Therefore comfort one another with these words.

Revelations 19:11-19

And I saw heaven opened, and behold, a white horse, and He who sat on it is called Faithful and True, and in righteousness He judges and wages war. His eyes are a flame of fire, and on His head are many diadems; and He has a name written on Him which no one knows except Himself. He is clothed with a robe dipped in blood, and His name is called The Word of God. And the armies which are in heaven, clothed in fine linen, white and clean, were following Him on white horses. From His mouth comes a sharp sword, so that with it He may strike down the nations, and He will rule them with a rod of iron; and He treads the wine press of the fierce wrath of God, the Almighty. And on His robe and on His thigh He has a name written, "KING OF KINGS, AND LORD OF LORDS." Then I saw an angel standing in the sun, and he cried out with a loud voice, saying to all the birds which fly in midheaven, "Come, assemble for the great supper of God, so that you may eat the flesh of kings and the flesh of commanders and the flesh of mighty men and the flesh of horses and of those who sit on them and the flesh of all men, both free men and slaves, and small and great." And I saw the beast and the kings of the earth and their armies assembled to make war against Him who sat on the horse and against His army.

2 Thessalonians 2:1-12

Now we request you, brethren, with regard to the coming of our Lord Jesus Christ and our gathering together to Him, that you not be quickly shaken from your composure or be disturbed either by a spirit or a message or a letter as if from us, to the effect that the day of the Lord has come. Let no one in any way deceive you, for it will not come unless the apostasy comes first, and the man of lawlessness is revealed, the son of destruction, who opposes and exalts himself above every so-called god or object of worship, so that he takes his seat in the temple of God, displaying himself as being God. Do you not remember that while I was still with you, I was telling you these things? And you know what restrains him now, so that in his time he will be revealed. For the mystery of lawlessness is already at work; only he who now restrains will do so until he is taken out of the way. Then that lawless one will be revealed whom the Lord will slay with the breath of His mouth and bring to an end by the appearance of His coming; that is, the one whose coming is in accord with the activity of Satan, with all power and signs and false wonders, and with all the deception of wickedness for those who perish, because they did not receive the love of the truth so as to be saved. For this reason God will send upon them a deluding influence so that they will believe what is false, in order that they all may be judged who did not believe the truth, but took pleasure in wickedness.

4. Which do you find yourself looking forward to the most? Why?

   - The Lord descends in the clouds.

   - A loud voice from the clouds. (1 Thessalonians 4)

   - The Trumpet call of God. (1 Thessalonians 4)

   - The dead in Christ will be resurrected.

   - The Rapture of living believers to be with Jesus. (1 Thessalonians 4:13-18)

   - The Judgment of God upon the Wicked of the earth. (Revelations 4-19)

   - The Judgment Seat of Christ. (1 Corinthians 5:10)

   - The revelation of the Anti-Christ. (2 Thess. 2)

- The visible appearance of Christ as Savior, Lord, and God to the whole world. (Matt. 24; 1 Thess. 4; 2 Thess. 1)

- The Millennial Kingdom of Christ. (Revelation 20:1-5; Isaiah 9:6)

Why?

_____

_____

_____

_____

5. If it is true that Jesus is coming back, are there things that you are doing that you don't want Jesus to come back while you are doing them?

- What are they?

- How are you going to stop doing those things?

6. Since it is true that Jesus is coming back, what are five things that you would like to have Christ find you doing when he comes back?

-

-

-

-

-

Round 3
Doctrinal Exercises

In this round of looking at the core doctrines of the Christian faith, we will be asking you to think of ten basic questions about each of the key Christian Doctrines. I've given you some examples in each category to get you started.

Day/Week 26

Questions about the Bible

1. How many books of the Bible are there?

2. What is each book really about?

3. How do we know that the Bible is the words of God and not just another book?

4.

5.

Day/Week 27

Questions about God

1. How do we know there is a God?

2. What is God like?

3. Why doesn't God just show himself to us?

4. How come there are so many different religions?

5. If God is all-powerful, why doesn't he fix our world?

Day/Week 28

Questions about Jesus

1. When was Jesus born?

2. Did Jesus exist before he was born?

3. Where is Jesus now?

4. What is Jesus doing now?

5. Why has he not come back? It has been a long time...

Day/Week 29

Questions about the Holy Spirit

1. What does the Holy Spirit do?

2. How can a Christian learn to hear the voice of the Holy Spirit?

3.

4.

5.

Day/Week 30

Questions about Mankind

1. What is the purpose for life?

2. Why did God create men and women?

3. How can humans create such beauty and good and also cause such pain, destruction, and evil?

4. If God created humanity innocent in a perfect environment, where did sin come from?

5.

Day/Week 31

Questions about Salvation

1. Isn't God supposed to forgive?

2. Why can't God just let everyone into heaven?

3. How can I take full advantage of God's salvation?

4. Is salvation about more than just going to heaven when I die?

5.

Day/Week 32

Questions about the Church

1. Why are there so many different Christian denominations and churches?

2. If everybody believes Christianity, why don't they all get together?

3. Why would the perfect God ask people to be a part of such an imperfect group called the church?

4.

5.

Day/Week 33

Questions about Angels

1. What are the two basic divisions of angels?

2. Do angels still manifest in our day? (Yes)

3. How many different kinds of angels are referred to in the Bible?

4. What do the different angels do?

5. Who is Satan?

6. What different kinds of evil angels are there?

7. Was there ever a time before there was evil?

Day/Week 34

Questions about the Afterlife: Judgment Day

1. What happens after you die?

2. How does God know what happened to us?

3. Why are Christians and non-Christians treated differently?

4. What is God looking for in the review of our life?

5.

Day/Week 35

Questions about the Afterlife: Heaven

1. What is so great about Heaven?

2. Won't we get bored after awhile?

3. Christians seem to believe in an unethical entrance means of getting into heaven. People will get in to heaven based upon who they know, not what they have done.

4. How can heaven be a place without evil? Won't that make it boring and rob it of choices and growth?

5.

Day/Week 36

Questions about the Afterlife: Hell

1. What is Hell like?

2. Which of the following descriptors has the most meaning for you and why?

3. Why would any enlightened person believe in an eternal hell?

4.

5.

Day/Week 37

Questions about the Return of Christ

1. How do we know Jesus is coming back?

2. When is he coming back?

3. What are the signs that he is getting ready to come back?

4. What should we do while we are waiting for him to come back?

5.

Round 4
Doctrinal Exercises

Day/Week 38

God

Which of these aspects of God that are represented in his names do you need in your life right today? Pick three.

Tell the people in your group.
Tell God...

EL: God, mighty, strong, prominent (Genesis 7:1)

ELOHIM: God as Creator, Preserver, Transcendent, Mighty and Strong (Genesis. 17:7, 6:18, 9:15, 50:24; 1 Kings 8:23)

EL SHADDAI: God is All-Sufficient, Lord God the Almighty (Genesis 17:1,2; Revelation 16:7)

ADONAI: Lord in our English Bibles (First use of Adonai, Genesis 15:2; 2 Samuel 7:18-20)

JEHOVAH: Yahweh is the covenant name of God. From the verb "to be", havah, similar to chavah (to live), "The Self-Existent One." (Exodus 3)

JEHOVAH-JIREH: The Lord will Provide (Genesis 22:14)

JEHOVAH-ROPHE: The Lord Who Heals (Exodus 15:22-26)

JEHOVAH-NISSI: The Lord Our Banner (Exodus 1:15)

JEHOVAH-M'KADDESH: The Lord Who Sanctifies; To make whole, set apart for holiness. (Leviticus 20:8)

JEHOVAH-SHALOM: The Lord Our Peace; Shalom translated "peace" 170 times means "whole," "finished," "fulfilled." (Judges 6:24)

SHEPHERD: (Psalm 23, Genesis 49:24; Isaiah. 40:11)

JUDGE: (Psalm 96:13)

JEHOVAH ELOHIM: LORD God (Genesis 2:4)

JEHOVAH-TSIDKENU: The Lord Our Righteousness (Jeremiah 23:5, 6, 33:16)

JEHOVAH-ROHI: The Lord Our Shepherd (Psalm 23)

JEHOVAH-SHAMMAH: The Lord is There (Ezekiel 48:35)

JEHOVAH-SABAOTH: The Lord of Hosts; The commander of the angelic host and the armies of God. (Isaiah 1:24; 2 Kings 3:9-12)

EL ELYON: Most High (from "to go up") (Deuteronomy 26:19, 32:8; Psalm 18:13; Genesis 14:18)

ABHIR: Mighty One (Genesis 49:24; Deuteronomy 10:17)

KADOSH: Holy One (Psalm 71:22; Isaiah 40:25)

SHAPHAT: Judge (Genesis 18:25)

EL ROI: God of Seeing Hagar (Genesis 16:13)

KANNA: Jealous; zealous (Exodus 20:5, 34:14)

PALET: Deliverer (Psalm 18:2)

YESHA: Y'shua; Savior (Isaiah 43:3)

GAOL: Redeemer (Job 19:25)

MAGEN: Shield (Psalm 3:3, 18:30)

EYALUTH: Strength (Psalm 22:19)

TSADDIQ: Righteous One (Psalm 7:9)

EL-OLAM: God of Everlasting Time (Gen. 21:33; Ps 90:1-3)

EL-GIBHOR: Mighty God (Isaiah 9:6)

ZUR: God our Rock (Deuteronomy 32:18; Isaiah 30:29)

THE SUN OF RIGHTEOUSNESS: (Malachi 4:2)

ATTIQ YOMIN: Ancient of Days (Daniel 7:9)

MELEKH: King (Psalm 5:2, 29:10, 44:4, 47:6-8)

THE ANGEL OF THE LORD: (Genesis 16:7ff, 21:17, Exodus 3:6, 13:21)

FATHER: (2 Samuel 7:14-15)

THE FIRST AND LAST: (Isaiah 44:6, 48:12)

Day/Week 39

Jesus

1. Which of the following names of Jesus has he been for you in the last three months?

2. Give praise to the Lord Jesus that he is and successfully fulfilled his mission of redemption.

3. Ask him to open your eyes to see these various aspects of who he is and what he does.

4. Yield to Christ in these various roles and ministries in your life:

New Testament Scriptures

KURIOS: "Lord"

DESPOTES: "Lord" (Luke 2:29; Acts 4:24)

THEOS: "God"

"I AM": From the Hebrew OT verb "to be" signifying a Living, Intelligent, Personal Being (John 8:58)

THEOTES: "Godhead" (Colossians 2:9; Romans 1:20)

HUPSISTOS: "Highest" (Matthew 21:9)

SOTER: "Savior" (Luke 1:47)

JESUS: From the Hebrew "Joshua" meaning JEHOVAH IS SALVATION

CHRIST: equivalent to the Hebrew 'Messiah' (Meshiach), "The Anointed One"

Other New Testament Titles for Jesus

SHEPHERD OF THE SHEEP

MASTER

KING OF KINGS

LORD OF LORDS

BISHOP AND GUARDIAN OF OUR SOULS

DAYSTAR

DELIVERER

ADVOCATE

SECOND ADAM

ANCIENT OF DAYS

BRANCH

CHIEF CORNERSTONE

IMMANUEL

FIRST BORN

HEAD OF THE BODY

PHYSICIAN

ROCK

ROOT OF JESSE

STONE

CHIEF APOSTLE

GREAT HIGH PRIEST

PIONEER AND PERFECTER OF OUR FAITH OR
AUTHOR AND FINISHER

LAMB OF GOD

LAMB SLAIN BEFORE THE FOUNDATION OF THE
WORLD

LORD GOD ALMIGHTY

LOGOS

SOPHIA

Day/Week 40

Holy Spirit

1. Give praise to the Holy Spirit that he is all these various roles and ministries.

2. Ask him to open your eyes to see these operating in, to, and for you.

3. Yield to the Holy Spirit in these various roles and ministries in your life. Which three do you sense that he is trying to minister to you right now?

Names for the Holy Spirit

COUNSELOR

COMFORTER

BAPTIZER

ADVOCATE

STRENGTHENER

SANCTIFIER

SPIRIT OF CHRIST

SEVEN-FOLD SPIRIT

SPIRIT OF TRUTH

SPIRIT OF GRACE

SPIRIT OF MERCY

SPIRIT OF GOD

SPIRIT OF HOLINESS

SPIRIT OF LIFE

Day/Week 41

Mankind

The Bible says that humanity has two significant aspects:

1. We were created in the image of God
2. We are broken and twisted by sin

Genesis 1:26

Then God said, "Let Us make man in Our image, according to Our likeness; and let them rule over the fish of the sea and over the birds of the sky and over the cattle and over all the earth, and over every creeping thing that creeps on the earth."

What does it mean to be created in God's image?

It means that each human individual is:

Wonderful, Significant, and Immortal

How have you and/or the people you know given evidence that they were created in the image of God within the last month?

Romans 3:23

...for all have sinned and fall short of the glory of God

What does it mean to say that man is sinful?

It means that each human individual is:
Selfish, Rebellious and Imperfect

How have you and/or the people you know given evidence that they are broken and twisted by sin within the last month?

Round 5
Developing a Christian Worldview

Day/Week 42

I have written down 10 implications of the Bible being the infallible, inerrant Word of God. React to these implications by writing in the space provided under each implication. Talk about your reaction with your small group.

1. I should pay attention to it. If the Bible is a message from God, then we should pay incredible amounts of attention to it. Read it every day. Is there some part of your life that is clearly out of line with what you know the Bible to teach? Change it as quickly as you can.

2. The Bible is the only reliable guide for the afterlife. There are many books and "experts" about what happens after we die, but only the Bible is a proven guide. Do not trust people or reports that do not agree with what the Bible says about the afterlife.

3. The Bible is a message from God on how to live life. The Bible does not tells us all that we would like to know, but it does tell us what we need to know. The Bible tells us how to live in relation to God. The Bible tells us how to be married, how to be a family, how to handle our money, how to become the best us we can be, how to develop a community of friends, how to maximize our work and career. Are there areas where you are not paying attention to what the Bible is

saying? Find a class and move your life in line with the Bible.

4. The Bible will never go out of date. Too often we read the paper or watch the news to know what is going on, but in 10 days we will have forgotten about everything we were paying so much attention to. But when we pay attention to the Bible, we are paying attention to truths, principles, and concepts that have stood the test of time for thousands of years and will continue to last when we are long into eternity.

5. The Bible is alive with the Spirit of God and becomes active in our soul. Scripture says that the Bible is a living book. Have you experienced a verse or phrase or chapter of the Bible grabbing you by the neck and making you pay attention because it so powerfully applies to your life? If you haven't then you have been reading it enough or reading it in a translation that will speak to you. Let the Bible speak, it is alive with the power of the Holy Spirit.

6. If I am not reading, studying, and meditating on the Bible every day, I am a fool. This is a message from God. Read the Psalms or the Proverbs every day and ask God for wisdom to guide your life for that day. It is always amazing how the timeless wisdom of God in the Bible speaks to the situations of life incredibly powerfully. Do not pay as much attention to the news; pay more attention to the Bible.

7. The Bible working in our minds does things to rewire and rework the way we think beyond what we can comprehend. Get it in there. I have known people who have fried their brains on drugs and yet through memorization and meditation on the Bible they have slowly rebuilt or rewired their brains to function well. I personally know that injecting heavy doses of the Bible in my mind every day and meditating on it has made my mind work differently than it would have without the Bible. God rewires and reworks our brains through biblical injections of truth.

8. Praying the Bible is the best way to know that you are praying the will of God. Open the Scriptures and begin asking for what God is talking about in that passage for yourself, for your loved ones, for you country, etc.

9. Don't be afraid of using the biblical truths in the modern world. You will be smarter than others and wiser than others when your ideas come out of biblical wisdom. We are often so interested in appearing current that we are actually spouting stupidity. Sometimes what is current is foolishness or sin repackaged in modern words. When the Bible says something is wrong, then it is wrong even if our society says it is good. The society's opinion is only a temporary phase until they realize that the Bible was right. Biblical wisdom has stood the test of time and always will even though culture, opinions, and empires change.

10. God gave us the truths we needed to know in written form so that we could not corrupt what He was saying. For thousands of years God has been speaking in various ways and yet we managed to mangle what He was saying. Beginning about 3,000-4,000 years ago He decided to communicate in written form. It is written so that we would not twist it and corrupt it, so don't do that, let the Bible say what it says.

Day/Week 43

I have written down 10 implications of the Creator God existing—the One who is above, beyond, and before any Being I can conceive. React to these implications by writing in the space provided under each implication. Talk about your reaction with your small group.

1. I can study nature and I am studying about God and what He did. For thousands of years Christians declared that there were two books about God: the Bible and the Book of Nature. Too often these days people do not realize and appreciate that when they are a biologist or a zoologist or some other kind of scientist, they are studying what God did. It is theology in a different way. There are many theories about how God did it.

2. God knows the beginning and ending of this universe. In the planning process of the universe, God knew and planned when it would start and when it would end. The various mysteries of the universe are not a mystery

3. I can only comprehend a very small part of the wonder that is God. It is clear that the author of the universe is a being who understands and manipulates physics and the laws of nature in ways that we are only now beginning to comprehend. The mysteries of other galaxies and the surprises that await discovery are

completely known to Him and unknown to us. The more we learn the more it is clear that we know only a small part of the vast sum of knowledge that presents itself to His infinite mind.

4. Planet Earth is a small blue space craft designed to house beings that God knew would become rebellious. It is interesting to pull back and realize that our planet is carrying life through the universe, and it has become rebellious life. God has isolated it in a remote part of the universe so that our rebellious creatures cannot make it to other solar systems while He accomplishes the redemption of those who are willing to repent.

5. I should live life God's way. Since God created everything and He created all the rules and laws by which everything works, it would make sense if I lived God's way. He has sent a manual on how to conduct our lives.

6. God has installed into life on this planet reproofs that let us know when we are no longer within His specified perimeters. When we don't sleep enough, we look horrible and feel sleepy all the time. When we don't handle our finances correctly, there is too much month left at the end of our money. When we treat people rude and offensively, we have bad relationships and less friends and joy. All over our lives God has installed rebukes and feedback loops if we would only pay attention to them. (Proverbs 1:22)

7. The only reasonable response to the beauty of a sunset or the wonder of the forests or a hike in the mountains is worship. We need to get outside of our churches and let the wonder of what God created call us to worship. Go find the part of nature that makes you worship and worship the God Creator.

8. It is only the arrogance and theories of men that hide the wonder of God's attributes and nature in the creation. People in every culture and society spin tales of why the wonder of creation should not push us to contemplate God and run to Him.

9. When I enjoy a run or a hike, I am enjoying the wonder of God. When I walk along the beach with my wife, we are doing what God intended. When I am fishing on a lake or backpacking in the woods, this is what God intended with His creation.

10. There is something rejuvenating and recalibrating about nature. We need it. I need to be around water and trees to be my authentic self. Get out there in the part of His creation that re-energizes you.

Day/Week 44

I have written down 10 implications of Jesus being the Son of God, Savior of the World, and Lord of all Lords. React to these implications by writing in the space provided under each implication. Talk about your reaction with your small group.

1. I should believe in him as God. We have lost the idea of what it really means to have someone be your God. But it means that they control the whole of your life. You exist within the boundaries of their will. Jesus thankfully wants us to flourish, but He does have boundaries on our behavior. We can do anything we want within His moral boundaries. These are clearly the Ten Commandments with His twists on them.

2. I should believe in him as my personal Savior. We -- as rebellious, selfish humans -- are facing the wrath of God for our arrogance and refusal to follow God's laws. Jesus is the one who has taken the wrath of God for us. If we respond to God's offer of Jesus, then we pass out of death into the forgiveness, life, and grace of God. It is astounding that Jesus would be willing to be our personal savior, but He offers Himself to us.

3. I should let him lead my life. Since Jesus is God and since He offers Himself as our personal Savior to escape the just penalty of our sins, He should lead our

life. We should allow Him to guide our life. If there are any areas where we are not allowing Him to lead and direct in our lives, we should change that.

4. I should serve Christ. Jesus Christ has served us through His perfect life and sacrificial death. He continues to serve us by praying for us and interceding for us as we live our lives. We should serve Him in our world. It is not our life any more; it is His to direct. What does He want you to do? How does He want you to serve? It is important to say that only a small portion of Christians should become pastors and missionaries; but all Christians should serve Him at their work, in their neighborhoods, in their marriages and parenting, and in their communities of faith.

5. I should worship Christ. Bowing down to Christ is a way of humbling ourselves and ascribing the right amount of honor and majesty to Jesus the Christ. Sometimes we are not specific enough in our worship and we just sing to God in general. It is appropriate to stop and sing worship songs to Jesus. To speak praise to Jesus the Christ. To write poems of worship to Jesus.

6. Jesus is the supreme human who ever lived. Get to know Him through reading or listening to His story in the gospels again. Get one of the audio versions of the Bible in a very understandable translation and listen to just the gospels and let the story of Jesus roll over you. Let yourself be there on the beaches of the Sea of Galilee with the disciples. Sit by the mantle of the

houses that Jesus is in and listen to Him tells the stories that educated His disciples.

7. Jesus is our High Priest and we can approach Him with every thought and every concern. He has been tempted in all points like we are, but He did not sin. He has felt the pain of loss. He has known the sting of rejection. He understands the pressure of time. Go on a walk and talk with Him about whatever is on your mind. Pull up an empty chair and tell Him the troubles of your life as you would your most trusted counselor because that is what He is.

8. Since Jesus is the Son of God and the Savior and the Lord of heaven and earth, we should listen again to how He wants us to live our lives. Read the Sermon on the Mount and let the truth of Jesus' words instruct you. This was for His disciples. It is not an impossible list of things that must wait for heaven. Let Jesus instruct you and the Holy Spirit guide you as you listen to Jesus teach in the Sermon on the Mount.

9. Jesus is coming back. Are you ready? Is there any part of your life that you would not want Jesus to find you doing when He comes back? Read the Olivet Discourse (Matthew 24, 25) and let Jesus tell you about His return. Live in the light of His return.

10. The Apostle John tells us that one-day we will be glorified because we will see Jesus face to face. Won't that be amazing? The final realization of our adoption into the forever family of God will be complete. We will have all that is sinful and rebellious eliminated, and we will be fitted for heaven. What will you want to ask Jesus? What will you want to do with the Lord Jesus in heaven? Are there areas that have resisted the work of Jesus right now that you know He will purify on that wonderful day when you see Him face to face?

Day/Week 45

I have written down 10 implications of the Holy Spirit being God and the manifest presence of Christ in my life. React to these implications by writing in the space provided under each implication. Talk about your reaction with your small group.

1. I should cooperate with the ministries of the Holy Spirit in my life.

2. I should find out my spiritual gift and build a large portion of my life around using this spiritual gift for the advancement of Christ's kingdom.

3. I should not grieve the Holy Spirit.

4. I should pay attention when the Holy Spirit prompts me.

5. I should let God the Holy Spirit flow through me to produce the fruit of the Spirit in my life.

6. God the Holy Spirit has given me at least one gift and usually a few. I should find out what these special abilities are and how to benefit the church with them.

7. Having the Spirit of Christ with us is a better helper than having Jesus Christ be present in one spot on the earth with 24 hours everyday availability. We are so often materialistic that we do not take full advantage of the presence of the Holy Spirit. He does want to direct us.

8. The Bible says that those who are believers will hear a voice behind them saying, "This is the way; walk in it." "Do not turn to the right or the left."

9. The presence of the Holy Spirit is the engagement ring from the Lord Jesus Christ. It is evidence that we are engaged to a wonderful husband. It is proof that He is coming back for us.

10. If we are not enjoying the presence of the Holy Spirit, we are missing out on one of the best gifts the Lord Jesus gives on this earth.

Day/Week 46

I have written down 10 implications of each man and woman being a tri-partite being made in the Image of God as well as sinful and broken. React to these implications by writing in the space provided under each implication. Talk about your reaction with your small group.

1. I should expect people to be selfish and sinful toward me. This contagion has spread to everyone. There is none that is righteous; no not one.

2. People are a mixture of dissimilar properties. This is why they are able as a species to produce such soaring creativity and such devastating evil. They are made as image bearers of the God. They are also permanently flawed and bent on selfishness, rebellion, and pride.

3. I should treat people with the dignity that their status as image bearers of God deserves. Everyone I meet is my teacher and superior in some way. They have a soul and are valuable.

4. To be an image bearer of God Almighty means that we are wonderful, significant, and immortal. We are not just the dirt and chemical elements that make up our

body. We have an eternal spirit and soul. What we are, what we choose, and what we become will continue to exist forever.

5. I should make sure that I feed my soul and my spirit, not just my physical body. Our materialistic world puts way too much emphasis on the physical and neglects the spiritual part of who we are as humans. Each person must feed their soul and spirit just as they stop three times a day and feed their body.

6. I have been made to reflect the image of God and give him glory. My significance and impact in the world is how often I do this. I am not being judged by how strong my impact is but how Christ-like my life becomes.

7. God displayed His glory through creativity. I can also reflect His glory when I do that creative thing that I was made to do whether that is gardening, woodworking, photography, building companies, or making films.

8. When I do not use the gifts and abilities that God has given me, then I rob the world and God of what He wanted me to do.

9. We must realize that almost everyone we meet has their default-setting stuck on selfishness and self-focus. We should not be surprised if they only want to talk about themselves, do what they want, and try not to notice that there are consequences.

10. Our spirit, soul, and body will be redeemed by the Lord our God. There is no part of mankind that is by nature wicked and unredeemable. We will be given a new body in heaven which will do many new things but which will share some aspects of the old body.

Day/Week 47

I have written down 10 implications of God's salvation being provided through Christ to the World. React to these implications by writing in the space provided under each implication. Talk about your reaction with your small group.

1. God loves me. It is obvious from the Old and New Testaments. He has been looking for people who would believe in Him and follow Him. He did all this planning, creating, and working with people because of people like me who would choose to love Him.

2. God wants my imperfect worship. While God must have far superior worship in heaven from the angels, he wants my worship.

3. God wants a relationship with me. He was willing to work through all the difficulties and process of sending His Son to die for my salvation. It is amazing that He wants to save me, but He does.

4. God wants my cooperation with his program (for my sake). God does not need my cooperation, but He offers to give me a great life if I would embrace the whole of His salvation process.

5. Because of all that God has done when I am in Christ I have no more condemnation that is hanging over me.

6. God set in motion a plan for my forgiveness before the world began. He is not surprised by my sin and brokenness.

7. I need to work out the salvation that God has provided for me in Jesus Christ. It is my loss if I allow aspects of His salvation to remain dormant in my life.

8. God is still working on me and through me, and I become better at this thing called being a Christian by loving God more and loving others more.

9. There will be a part of salvation that will not be completed until I see Jesus Christ face to face. He will complete me and bring me fully to the state where I can enter heaven with Him.

10. God has given me a whole new life. I don't need to respond the way I have in the past to the pressures, temptations, irritations, and problems. I have died and my life is hidden with Christ in God. I can drop below my old systems and rise above them to live with new habits and new responses.

Day/Week 48

I have written down 10 implications of the church being God's creation for believers and the promoter of God's glory and the gospel. React to these implications by writing in the space provided under each implication. Talk about your reaction with your small group.

1. Everyone needs a Christian community to accomplish their spiritual journey. I cannot just be a spiritual person without a community of Christians encouraging me. If I try that, I am doomed to a weak or lost faith.

2. The church is not about meeting an individual's needs. The reason I go to church is not so that my needs will be met but so that I will be in community. It is that community that will worship God, meet other people's needs, bring significance, relationships, and meet my needs.

3. God has provided a community for you to thrive and become a loving and giving Christian. Yes there will be people at every church that will irritate you and force you out of your comfort zone. This is supposed to happen, and it will expand your ability to love.

4. The church is not just a club for Christians but is to be welcoming new Christians and guiding seekers at all times. Too often churches become little clubs for people who think alike and have the same interests. If a church is not bringing new people to faith on a regular basis, then it is unhealthy.

5. The church is supposed to be about life change. It is not okay to go to a church for years and be the same person. People should be transformed by their experience at church. Is that happening to you at your church?

6. Churches have different styles but should clearly worship God. There are lots of ways to worship and singing is only one of the ways. There is something powerful that happens when God's people worship collectively.

7. God give gifts to Christians so that they could help be the church to each other and to the watching world. This means that the teachers should teach, the leaders should lead, the merciful should comfort and so on. If you are a Christian you have at least one gift. Are you using it?

8. Fellowship is a sharing in common with others. If true fellowship is going to happen in church, then people must unzip their souls to one another in their

community of faith. Your Christian community must be safe enough to do that. It must be interested in you as a person, not just you as a attender or tither.

9. Being in a healthy church is messy. The church when it is serving Jesus asks you to serve. It asks you to go beyond your comfort zone. It asks you to be a part of a vulnerable community of friends. It asks you to talk with and help those who are really different than you. Be a part of the church, not just attend one.

10. The community of faith has always been a generous place. It is where people who are afflicted, oppressed, and wounded can come and receive real help. The church cannot just hope people get better; it has to help raise up leaders for the issues of our time. It must send volunteers to help make a difference. It must be a voice for morality when evil and destruction are accepted. Becoming a part of a healthy church means that you become a generous person in your soul.

Day/Week 49

I have written down 10 implications of Angels being sent to minister to those who are being saved and some being allowed to tempt, plague, disrupt, and attack people. React to these implications by writing in the space provided under each implication. Talk about your reaction with your small group.

1. I can expect to be harassed and disrupted when I am doing a righteous thing because there are wicked spiritual beings who do not want righteousness to go forward. This is called spiritual warfare.

2. I am being sent unseen spirit beings (angels) to help me accomplish God's will for my life. If you have ever seen or sensed that you had an encounter with one, tell the story.

3. God is watching my life and will send help. When I pray God sends help in many different forms. Sometimes it is angelic in nature.

4. There is a whole host of wicked spirits who are watching me and looking for my weaknesses and susceptibility to sin. They have to follow God's laws and rules. They do not have free shots at us unless we

are living outside of the 10 Commandments, unless God specifically grants it so we can grow and deepen.

5. I am in a spiritual war. In a sense I am behind enemy lines on this rebel planet. God wants me to listen to His Word and His Spirit to live a righteous life and help rescue people that God is calling to repentance.

6. God asks me to fight for what is right and equips me with what I need to win the war. I have been given the Armor of God and all the other Weapons of Righteousness. Every time I do a righteous thing, I strike a blow for the righteousness of God's kingdom.

7. I will lose some battles. There will be some times when I am led into testing and I will fail. But I don't have to stay there. In Christ's power I can jump back into the fight. God is ready to hear my confession to Him and forgive me.

8. Don't get caught up by angels and demons. They are a part of the universe that God created. Our job is to live righteously and serve the Lord our God. Yes, there are angels and, yes, there are demons, but the real wonder is God.

9. The Devil corrupted himself by wanting more than the amazing assignment God had given him. He filled up his soul with pride and was judged for his pride and rebellion.

10. There are millions of holy angels that exist to serve the Lord in various capacities. This spiritual side to life can not be ignored if we are to truly understand all that is happening in our world.

Day/Week 50

I have written down 10 implications of an Afterlife: Judgment Day specifically. React to these implications by writing in the space provided under each implication. Talk about your reaction with your small group.

1. Our culture has lost track of Judgment Day when we will all be judged for everything we did, said, thought, emoted and the motive for our actions. Just because we don't think about it doesn't mean that it isn't going to happen. Our culture's trust in naturalism's lie that when we die it is all over has put most people to sleep about the coming evaluation of everything they did.

2. I determine what the Lord Jesus Christ will be looking for in my life on Judgment Day. He will either be looking for every mistake, sin, and evil I did; or He will be looking for anything I did with and through His power.

3. My choice is to either pay for my sins on my own or to accept the gracious offer of the death of Christ on Calvary for all my sins and receive His perfection to my account. (Even my ability to choose is a gift from God, but God counts my faith as righteousness).

4. There are two verses that make me think that the people who we talked about will be invited to see and hear the tape of our life. One verse says that every hidden thing will be made known and the second one is that every idle word will be brought into judgment. The only way that can happen is if the people who we talk about are able to see what we really think and what we really said about them. It will all come out so live a life of love. This is also a reason why we need Jesus to pay for our sins and selfishness.

5. For those who have accepted Jesus as their Christ and as their Savior, they pass out of the judgment of life and death and move into a judgment for rewards. In this judgment Jesus is looking for each time you trusted Christ, each time you allowed God's power to flow through you to do a good thing, each time you gave glory to God through what you said and did.

6. Every generation of people worldwide for all of recorded history has understood that they will be facing judgment when they die except this last generation that has believed the lie of secular naturalism. Who do you think will be right?

7. I should accept Jesus' forgiveness for me and his leadership in my life so that I will be at the judgment for rewards.

8. I should warn people to accept Jesus and flee from the wrath of God by running to the forgiveness that is in Christ because judgment day is real.

9. We are not judged on the size of our impact but the amount and times that we let God flow through us.

10. Everyone has the same chance for rewards because every minute is a minute that we can be trusting Christ and living for Him.

Day/Week 51

I have written down 10 implications of an Afterlife in Heaven where intimacy with God, rest, significant service, and removal of pain are realities. React to these implications by writing in the space provided under each implication. Talk about your reaction with your small group.

1. I should anticipate heaven and the rewards that will come there. There are things I will have to sacrifice here because I know that heaven will more than make up for whatever I pass up to help others here.

2. I should accept Jesus Christ's forgiveness so that I can go to heaven. It is not possible to be good enough to earn your way to heaven. You have to have help. You have to have God supply everything.

3. I should make as much progress in my faith and service to God in this life so that I will be trusted with more responsibility in heaven. Jesus clearly ties what we will be doing in heaven with how we trusted and served Him here.

4. Clearly the life we are now living is a warm up for the next one. What we do here determines what we are allowed to do there. This trial run perspective on life here has largely been lost because of the naturalistic philosophy that surrounds us.

5. God can at any time emerge from behind the veil of heaven and take us into eternity. There is no guarantee that we will live 70-80 years. Whenever God decides that a person's eternal future has been determined then He can move that person out of this temporary existence.

6. The picture of heaven that emerges from Revelation 21 and Revelation 22 as well as the other places in Scripture is one of intimate communion with God and real work serving God in various capacities. There will be assignments to accomplish and things to trust God for in heaven. We will not spend eternity celebrating, remembering, or bemoaning what we did in the few years here on earth.

7. God deals with our past here on earth and wipes away our tears and perfects our weaknesses, but the focus in not on the past but the future we will have in serving God.

8. We are now citizens of heaven and should act like it. We are willing to sacrifice things here because we know that they do not matter there. We are willing to do things here because we understand that they have great meaning there. The only way that the early church could "joyfully accept the seizure of their property" was the knowledge that heaven is real and the rewards of heaven are far greater than anything we experience here.

9. The Bible tells us to study heaven and act like ambassadors of that country. It is very easy to be selfish and grasping for this world, but it proves that we do not understand the next one. We have the privilege of learning to love in this world and in that way show we understand the next one.

10. Heaven will be a place of answers and of new growth and new information. What questions do you want to ask Jesus? From what you see in Revelation 21 and Revelation 22 what structures, knowledge, and information do you think you will be exposed to in heaven that you don't have here?

Day/Week 52

I have written down 10 implications of an Afterlife in Hell where people will be eternally regretting the selfish decisions they made and the injurious choices and actions that they took. React to these implications by writing in the space provided under each implication. Talk about your reaction with your small group.

1. Hell is the temporary containment unit for those who have chosen a selfish path and refused to accept the forgiveness, dependence, and relationship with God through Jesus Christ.

2. People in Hell will continue to grow more and more selfish throughout eternity. If you gave free reign to your selfishness and it continued to grow through thousands of years, what would you be capable of?

3. The upper compartment of Hell (Abraham's bosom, the place of the righteous dead who were waiting for Jesus' redemption) has been emptied by the life, death, resurrection, and ascension of Jesus Christ. Who are you looking forward to seeing in heaven who was at one time in the upper compartment of Hell.

4. Eventually at the end of history, Hell and death are emptied into the Lake of Fire. This eternal containment unit that was originally designed for the Devil and his wicked angels will be full. They need to be contained because they will continue to want to rebel, continue to want to be selfish, continue to want to destroy. In the Lake of Fire they will be confined and unable to harm anyone outside of the containment unit.

5. Each person is an eternal being and will go on directing their lives toward positive or negative goals for the whole of their existence, which is why Hell and the Lake of Fire exist. It is also why heaven exists. Each is designed to allow eternal beings to pursue their chosen course and reap the benefits and/or consequences of those chosen courses.

6. No one who gets away with evil in this world will escape the judgment of God in the next. He who knows the end from the beginning will be the one who examines a person. Ultimately everyone has been given two choices: throw themselves on the mercy of the court or continue their self-focused and self-sufficient ways.

7. I should implore people to turn from their wickedness because Hell is real and the Lake of Fire is forever.

8. I should cling closely to Christ and his forgiveness for me as I know that I deserve the fires and torments of Hell just as much as anyone who will actually end up there.

9. I should worship the righteous and all-wise God who will not allow the wicked to go unpunished. Nor will he punish the innocent for someone else's deeds and choices.

10. I will rejoice in the fact that even if a person gets away with evil in this life, they will not escape the judgment of God in the next life.

Day/Week 53

I have written down 10 implications of the Return of Christ to this earth as Warrior King of the Universe. React to these implications by writing in the space provided under each implication. Talk about your reaction with your small group.

1. Just as the promises of the first coming were fulfilled, so the promises of the second coming will be fulfilled.

2. Jesus is coming back for me.

3. Right before Jesus' return, the devil will be given much more room to deceive, damage, and destroy. When I see these and other signs, I need to increase my faith and be ready for Christ's return.

4. When he comes back, if I am alive, I will be changed into a different person physically, emotionally, mentally, and spiritually. I will be more connected to Christ and His mission.

5. I should be ready for his return. What would make me ready for the return of Christ? Are there people I need

to forgive? Are there people I need to treat with kindness? Are there service projects I have always meant to get to?

6. I should stop doing anything I would be ashamed of his catching me doing. Should I stop yelling? Should I stop looking at porn? Should I stop being dismissive of certain people? Should I eliminate swearing?

7. I should make sure that I am doing the things that I know he wants me to be doing.

8. I should not be frantic about his return but fulfilling my role in his kingdom advancement.

9. As God the Father and the Holy Spirit prepare to send Jesus back to earth for the second time, there will be a period of great Tribulation for those on the earth. Many will be deceived into following false Christ's.

10. When Jesus comes back to rule and reign, most people on the planet will not welcome His return but instead will resist His return. Millions and even billions of people will not want the Lord Jesus Christ to assume His rightful place as ruler of the world. They will seek to fight against the King of Kings.

Appendix 1
Verses for a Solid Christian Worldview

The Bible	2 Timothy 3:16; Psalm 19:7-11; 1 Peter 1:20-21
God	Exodus 34:6-7; Psalm 139:7-12; Acts 17:24-25; Exodus 3:13-15
Jesus	Isaiah 9:6; Luke 1:31-33; Revelation 1:17-18
Holy Spirit	Acts 5:3-5; Isaiah 11:2; John 16:7-14
Man: Sinful/Redeemed	Genesis 1:26-27; Romans 3:10-18; 1 Thessalonians 5:23
Salvation	John 1:29; Romans 8:28-30; Jeremiah 31:31-34
Church	Matthew 16:16-19; Acts 2:41-47; Ephesians 4:11-16
Angels: Good/Evil	Hebrews 1:14; Luke 2:13; Matthew 18:10; Ezekiel 28:12-19
Heaven; Hell; Judgment Day	Revelation 7:16,17; 21:1-22; 10; Luke 16:19-31; 2 Thessalonians 1:9; Matthew 25:41; Revelation 20:11-15; 2 Thess. 1:5-10; Daniel 12:2-3
The Return of Christ	Matt. 24.29-31; 1 Thessalonians 4:13-18; 2 Thess. 2:1-12; Revelations 19:11-16

Appendix 2

The Disciplines of Repetition

Biblical Meditation

We have done a fairly extensive look at three sections of Scripture, but it is always helpful to meditate on the biblical verses yourself. Therefore I have included this overview of the techniques of biblical meditation and the blank meditation worksheets to allow you to ruminate over these passages yourself. I have included ten blank sheets so that you can try all the various biblical techniques on each passage. I can remember my youth pastor always wanting ten pages of biblical meditation worksheets. He wanted me to press the Scriptures through every part of who I was: my spirit, my mind, my will, my emotions, and even my body. You never know which of the techniques will unlock an insight, a connection to God, a new application.

People are talking about meditation these days as though it were the sole property of the Eastern religions. Eastern religions practice a form of meditation. Using broad general categories, there are two types of meditation: **emptying forms** of meditation and **content-based forms** of meditation. All meditation is the focused attention of the mind upon something. In emptying forms of meditation, the mind is focused on a nonsense idea, word, phrase, or a logical absurdity in order to attempt an escape from the present space-time logical constraints. In content-based meditation the mind is focused on some form of content. There are three forms of content-based meditation: materialistic, spiritual, and biblical. Biblical meditation is "content-based" meditation with biblical words, ideas, phrases, and precepts as the meditated content. The new biblical qualities, reactions, and ideas will become a part of the person who is being shaped into Christ-likeness. The goal of the Christian is to have the Lord's thoughts become their thoughts (Isaiah 55:6-8, Psalm 1:1-3; Colossians 3:16; Joshua 1:8; Philippians 4:8; Deuteronomy 6:6-9).

The Incredible Power of Biblical Meditation

The most powerful form of transformational life-change known to man is meditation. In fact, no long-term life-change can take place without this meditation. The tragedy in Christian circles is that this powerful method is often unknown, unused, and in some cases even reviled. Biblical meditation was common practice in the Christian church for 1900 years. Yet in the last 150 years, biblical meditation has been left behind in the modern church as it searches for newer programs and crowd-pleasing techniques. The prophet Amos tells of a time when there will be a famine in the land: *Not a famine for bread, or a thirst for water, but rather for hearing the words of the Lord.* (Amos 8:11) We are living out a fulfillment of that vision. More Bibles are printed than ever before and yet the power of the Bible is not connecting with the souls of God's people. All the power people want for transformational life-change is near but remains untapped.

What is Biblical Meditation?

The idea behind biblical meditation is taken from a sheep or cow chewing its cud. The animal chews the grass and works it into a mush and then swallows it. It then brings it back up later to chew it some more. It repeats this process until all the nutrients have been extracted from the grass. Meditation is murmuring or repeating the concepts, ideas, and words of Scripture to extract all the richness and wisdom.

Biblical meditation is referred to in a number of ways in the Scriptures: delighting in Scripture (Psalm 119:16, 34, 47, 70); delighting in the Lord (Psalm 37:4); letting the Word of God richly dwell in your soul (Colossians 3:16); setting your mind on things above (Colossians 3:1); setting your mind on the Spirit (Romans 8:6); renewing your mind (Romans 12:2).

What Are the Techniques of Biblical Meditation?

Down through the centuries of Judeo-Christian history strong believers have discovered a number of methods for "chewing" Scripture. These techniques move the believer significantly forward in their pursuit of God and attainment of Christ-like living. The following list is not meant to be exhaustive or prioritized. Some will find certain techniques more helpful than others.

Confessionalize Scripture

To confessionalize Scripture is to take the Bible through your will. It is the process of comparing your life with the biblical standard and asking God whether this is true of your life. Every phrase or sentence of Scripture forms a way of examining your life.

First, each truth or action exposed in that Scripture is confessed as true and important. "Dear Lord, I agree with you that Christians should love one another."

Second, each truth or action is confessed as something you are doing or something that you are not doing. "Dear Lord, I freely admit that I am having a very difficult time loving this person right now. I know that I should, but I do not. Create in me a heart of love for this person." Or, "Dear Lord, I am encouraged to say that I am acting in a loving way toward my wife. I thank you for teaching me how to love her." Specifically and openly comparing your life with Scripture is a powerful way to draw the Bible through your will.

Visualize Scripture

The idea of biblical mediation through visualization is to take a passage of Scripture and make it come to life in your mind. It can be referred to as making a mental picture or movie of a biblical scene or concept. For thousands of years all societies have declared the power of the mind to shape behavior and achievement. There are at least two kinds of Scripture to visualize: narrative and didactic.

Narrative visualization is where one sees a biblical story actually taking place. Smelling the smells; hearing the sounds around the event; touching the equipment or clothing of the individuals in the story. In narrative meditation there needs to be focused attention on the biblical detail and an educated imagination to fill out the narrative storyline.

The second type of visualization is **didactic visualization**. This is where one pictures the truth of Scripture being lived out in present reality. When this is applied to doctrinal aspects of Scripture, the doctrinal truths are pictured. One might recognize the unseen hand of God moving on, in, and through the men who penned the Scripture to keep it error free and accurate. When this is applied to a practical principle for living, the principle is viewed as being lived out in life, such as being gentle in response to a sarcastic remark as in Proverbs 15:1. The key idea here is to actually picture oneself living out a scriptural concept. What has to be done to get in a position to live this biblical idea? If you can't see yourself doing a righteous idea in your mind, you will never do it. You have to see it before you will do it.

One of the clearest examples of this type of meditation is in Colossians 3:1-14. The apostle orders Christians to "set your minds on the things above;" "Put to death your earthly members: fornication, impurity, etc;" "Put on a heart of compassion, kindness, humility…" Each of these commands is a mental exercise designed to cause you to "occ" what is not your present experience. We are to see ourselves enjoying the wonders of heaven, intimacy with God, the qualities of Christ, entering into the heavenly economy, etc. We are to picture ourselves as unresponsive and unaffected by those temptations that are the most powerful in our lives. We are to make a mental movie of the qualities of Christ being our normal lifestyle. Mental movie-making of biblical ideas is God's way of renewing our minds.

Personalize Scripture

Personalizing Scripture can bring the power of an individual Scripture directly into your emotions. This technique is accomplished by inserting your name or a personal pronoun into a verse when saying it. One of the reasons that the Psalms are such a popular section of the Scripture is that in many cases they are already personalized. Years ago I was counseling a woman who was really having a hard time staying in her marriage. She wanted to end her marriage and pursue her selfish desires. I asked her to pray and ask God what she should do. She began praying and God began to bring back into her mind the Scriptural directions for wives in Ephesians 5 with her name woven through the commands. This was immensely powerful. "God spoke to me," she said. "He spoke to me and I will never forget it." This time of prayerful meditation was a turning point in her life. She went back home and threw herself into her marriage with new hope and determination. Her marriage improved dramatically because God had spoken through Scripture as it was being personalized to her.

Record Insights

Usually during the time when you are using the other methods of biblical meditation you will become aware of ancillary questions, insights, connections, or bits of wisdom that are in some ways connected to the Scripture but may not be the main points of the passage. These are called insights. It is as though God begins to open the Scriptures to you and the levels of wisdom contained within it. Christians have usually found that if they write down insights as they are meditating, then they receive more of these insights. It is almost like saying to God, "I'm paying attention." Sometimes this is called spiritual journaling. A meditation journal is a helpful way of recording your reactions, thoughts, insights, and promptings during meditation.

Pray Scripture

This technique is to turn the actual phrases of Scripture into prayers. It is very educational to pray God's desires back to Him. As your mind seeks ways to turn various passages into requests, you will uncover new angles and depth of understanding on the will of God. In every passage there are many different ways to turn the truths into prayer requests. This type of prayer resembles the Apostle Paul's prayers in Ephesians 1:18-21 and Ephesians 3:14-21. Asking for scriptural realities is often the best kind of praying for it keeps us from asking from a limited materialistic perspective. When we verbalize what God wants us to desire, we see the stark contrast between God's desires for us and our own fleshly desires.

Harmonize

There are at least two ways to meditate on Scripture through song. One is to sing the actual words of Scripture and adjust the tune to work with the unaltered words of the biblical text. The second method for meditating on Scripture through song is to take the truths, ideas, or concepts of the Scripture and sing those. This is a little easier and more free-flowing. When singing the Scripture it does not matter if it is great music, just that you are expressing the truths, feelings, and desires of Scripture. You will laugh, smile, ponder, and re-commit to the Lord as you sing the words or concepts of Scripture. It is really an enjoyable process, but it takes a little courage to get started.

Open the Bible, pick a tune you know, and begin singing the words of Scripture to the tune. Another way to harmonize the Scripture is to look at a passage or a Christian doctrine and write down three or four truths. Start making up a song about those truths. The tune and the words are changeable as long as they accurately reflect the truth of Scripture. Many of our great hymns and gospel songs have come from just such meditations. The writers were not trying to write great hymns but to express their heart and soul regarding the truths of God. "Amazing Grace" by John Newton, "Amazing Love" by Charles Wesley, and various versions of the Apostles Creed that have been set to music are all examples of this type of meditation.

What Are the Results of Biblical Meditation?

God makes some amazing promises in the Scripture regarding biblical meditation. In Joshua 1:8 and Psalm 1:1-3 God promises believers if they meditate on His law, they will be prosperous and successful. The mind filled with biblical principles and laws will avoid many of the hidden reefs that sink other people's lives. When a Christian purposefully fills their mind with Scripture, then the God of peace will move in and reassure that person that He is still in charge and He has a way through every storm. In Psalm 119:97-100, God promises believers that they will gain wisdom beyond their years if they meditate upon biblical concepts.

When Are the Best Times to Meditate?

God has specifically suggested particular times to ruminate on Scripture (Deuteronomy 6:6-9; Psalm 1:1-3; 4:4; 63:6). **First**, the Scripture says to meditate when we sit in our homes. This means that one must turn off the TV at times. Many business travelers would lessen the temptations of travel and increase intimacy with God by turning off the television when they travel. **Second**, the Scripture suggests that people should get into the habit of reorienting their minds to Scripture as they are going from place to place. This is a time to pre-plan the next appointment using biblical concepts and qualities. A **third** time to meditate on Scripture is right before going to sleep. As people focus their minds on the concepts, qualities, and words of Scripture right before they drift off to sleep, it allows their subconscious mind to embrace these concepts.

A **fourth** time to meditate each day is when the day begins. Many Christians set aside time each morning to spend extended time with God through biblical meditation. A **fifth** time for meditation is the night watches. These are times in the middle of the night spent with God and His Word.

The Disciplines of Repetition: Conclusion

Memorization and meditation are not the only disciplines of repetition, but they have for centuries formed two of the more crucial practices that develop the spiritual Christian. It is not enough merely to understand these practices; one must actually do them on a regular basis to impact the depths of the soul. The goal of memorization and meditation is to give God the Holy Spirit an ever-increasing supply of language and concepts to use when communicating with us. A third discipline of repetition is teaching. To use teaching as a discipline of repetition is to seek to explain what God has taught you. You don't have to be teacher and have gifts of teaching to teach. You just need to want to pass on the truths of the faith to others and in this way it will cement the truth to your own mind. My hope is that you will take the materials in this book and teach others in small groups -- one on one and the like.

Journal of Biblical Meditation

Scripture	
Slow Repetition	
Memorization	
Study	
Personalize	
Confessing	
Praying	
Envisioning	
Singing	
Journal Insights	
Diagramming/ Analogy	
Personal Translation	

Journal of Biblical Meditation

Scripture	
Slow Repetition	
Memorization	
Study	
Personalize	
Confessing	
Praying	
Envisioning	
Singing	
Journal Insights	
Diagramming/ Analogy	
Personal Translation	

Journal of Biblical Meditation

Scripture	
Slow Repetition	
Memorization	
Study	
Personalize	
Confessing	
Praying	
Envisioning	
Singing	
Journal Insights	
Diagramming/ Analogy	
Personal Translation	

Journal of Biblical Meditation

Scripture	
Slow Repetition	
Memorization	
Study	
Personalize	
Confessing	
Praying	
Envisioning	
Singing	
Journal Insights	
Diagramming/ Analogy	
Personal Translation	

Journal of Biblical Meditation

Scripture	
Slow Repetition	
Memorization	
Study	
Personalize	
Confessing	
Praying	
Envisioning	
Singing	
Journal Insights	
Diagramming/ Analogy	
Personal Translation	

Journal of Biblical Meditation

Scripture	
Slow Repetition	
Memorization	
Study	
Personalize	
Confessing	
Praying	
Envisioning	
Singing	
Journal Insights	
Diagramming/ Analogy	
Personal Translation	

Journal of Biblical Meditation

Scripture	
Slow Repetition	
Memorization	
Study	
Personalize	
Confessing	
Praying	
Envisioning	
Singing	
Journal Insights	
Diagramming/ Analogy	
Personal Translation	

Journal of Biblical Meditation

Scripture	
Slow Repetition	
Memorization	
Study	
Personalize	
Confessing	
Praying	
Envisioning	
Singing	
Journal Insights	
Diagramming/ Analogy	
Personal Translation	

Journal of Biblical Meditation

Scripture	
Slow Repetition	
Memorization	
Study	
Personalize	
Confessing	
Praying	
Envisioning	
Singing	
Journal Insights	
Diagramming/ Analogy	
Personal Translation	

Journal of Biblical Meditation

Scripture	
Slow Repetition	
Memorization	
Study	
Personalize	
Confessing	
Praying	
Envisioning	
Singing	
Journal Insights	
Diagramming/ Analogy	
Personal Translation	

About The Author

Gil Stieglitz is a catalyst for positive change both personally and organizationally. He excites, educates, and motivates audiences all over the world through passion, humor, leadership, and wisdom. He has led seminars in China, Europe, Canada, Mexico, and all over the United States.

Since founding the nonprofit ministry Principles to Live By in 1992 to help people and organizations win at life through Biblical Wisdom, Dr. Gil has been asked to repair, lead, and reinvigorate numerous organizations and individuals. He successfully led a church to 1400% growth in a disadvantaged area. As a Denominational Superintendent in the Western United States, he led 50 churches and 250 pastors to over 300% growth. As a Superintendent of Schools, he oversaw a school system as it doubled in 4 years. As an executive pastor at a mega-church, he rebuilt a staff and added over a 1,000 people. He injects dynamic life-change as a professor at universities and graduate schools on the West Coast and through seminars, sermons, and lecture series. He also partners with Courage Worldwide which rescues young girls who have been forced into sexual slavery in America.

He has a B.A. from Biola University and a Master's Degree and a Doctorate in Christian Leadership from Talbot School of Theology. He has authored over two dozen books, manuals, and development courses including three best sellers. Dr. Gil's resources are available at Amazon.com as well as at www.PrinciplesToLiveBy.com.

Gil and his wife, Dana, have enjoyed over twenty-five years of marriage and reside in Roseville, California, where they raised their three precious girls.

Other Resources by Gil Stieglitz

Becoming Courageous

Breakfast with Solomon Volume 1

Breakfast with Solomon Volume 2

Breakfast with Solomon Volume 3

Breaking Satanic Bondage

Deep Happiness: The Eight Secrets

Delighting in God

Delighting in Jesus

God's Radical Plan for Husbands

God's Radical Plan for Wives

Going Deep In Prayer: 40 Days of In-Depth Prayer

Leading a Thriving Ministry

Marital Intelligence

Mission Possible: Winning the Battle Over Temptation

Proverbs: A Devotional Commentary Volume 1

Proverbs: A Devotional Commentary Volume 2

Satan and the Origin of Evil

Secrets of God's Armor

Spiritual Disciplines of a C.H.R.I.S.T.I.A.N

The Schemes of Satan

They Laughed When I Wrote Another Book About Prayer, Then They Read It

Touching the Face of God: 40 Days of Adoring God

Why There Has to Be a Hell

Podcasts

Becoming a Godly Parent

Biblical Meditation: The Keys of Transformation

Everyday Spiritual Warfare Series

God's Guide to Handling Money

Spiritual War Surrounding Money

The Four Keys to a Great Family

The Ten Commandments

If you would be interested in having Gil Stieglitz speak to your group, you can contact Him through the website

www.ptlb.com